The Origin and Destiny of Humanity

William Earl Valentine Key-nee

Whitford Press

1469 Morstein Road
West Chester, Pennsylvania 19380 U.S.A.

The Origin and Destiny of Humanity
by William Earl Valentine Key-nee

Copyright © 1990 by William Earl Valentine Key-nee

Library of Congress Card Number: 89-051874
International Standard Book Number: 0-924608-00-5

Cover design by Bob Boeberitz
Cover illustration by Jon Wagner

Manufactured in the United States of America.

Published by Whitford Press,
a division of
Schiffer Publishing, Ltd.
1469 Morstein Road
West Chester, Pennsylvania 19380
Please write for a free catalog.
This book may be purchased from the publisher.
Please include $2.00 postage.
Try your bookstore first.

Acknowledgements

I was contemplating the inclusion of a standard bibliography with this manuscript. But when I sat down and the information contained within me rushed onto the pages, I knew that such a list of authors and publications would run into the hundreds, literally. I do wish to thank every scientist, philosopher, religionist, metaphysician, and so on that has added to this comprehensive perspective that I have laid out to the reader.

Those whose names I can recall, although they may not all have made an immense impact upon me as opposed to others not enumerated, are as follows: Anthony Fisichella, Alex Jones, Ralph Pestka, Dr. Gregory Little, Amy Wallace, Bill Henkin, Joseph Cater, Albert Roy Davis, Walter Rawls Jr., Anthony Norvell, Mark and Elizabeth Claire Prophet, Immanuel Velikovsky, John Keel, Robert Anton Wilson, Joseph Goodavage, Andrew Tomas, Dr. Ravi Batra, Jeremy Rifkin, Gene Roddenberry,

J.R. Jochmans, Guy Playfair, Scott Hill, Jon Klimo, William Irvin Thompson, Joseph Campbell, Tom Valentine, Donald Goldsmith, Gordon Strachan, John White, R. Roy Whitney, Stan Barker, Jeffrey Goodman, Louis Culling, Richard Noone, the Lusson Twins, Robert Theobald, Max Toth, Steven Halpern, Alan & Sally Landsburg, Erich von Daniken, Theodore Roszak, Peter Kolosimo, Linda Clark, Brad Steiger, Hilarion, Jacque Fresco, Manly Hall, Gene Savoy, Alvin and Heidi Toffler, Arthur C. Clarke, Buckminster Fuller, Robert K.G. Temple, Dr. Helen Wambach, Francie Steiger, Margaret Mead, Carl Llewelyn Weschcke, Richard Miller, Idres Shah, Elwood Babbitt, Stuart Wilde, Manson Valentine, Dan Baer, Charles Berlitz, Bill and Davina Cox, Mark DeMaranville, Auriloitha, Nikola Tesla, Budd Hopkins, Betty Hill, Jacques Vallee, Douglas Dean, Page Bryant, C.G. Jung, Barbara Marx Hubbard, Ilya Prigogine, Ruth Montgomery, Edgar Cayce, Nostradamus, Lazaris and Jach Pursel, Mircea Eliade, Jose Arguelles, Zecharia Sitchin, Marcel Vogel, Nigel Calder, Stephen J. Gould, Charles Fort, Rod Serling, Brit and Lee Elders, Billy Meier, the Urantia Foundation, plus all of the writers of the numerous religious texts that have been handed down to us through the centuries. Also, to all of the biologists, physicists, archaeologists, anthropologists, planetologists and those other arenas of science whose names I know I have left off this very short list. Without your work something would have been missing from the necessary multidimensional view leading to this monumental exposition.

Contents

Introduction

In order to truly understand why we are all here on Planet Earth and our place in the universe, we must embark on an unprecedented journey. This voyage will take us through various fields of study with a multidisciplinary approach. The end result will demonstrate how interconnected we are with the very universe itself.

It is clear to me that unless we possess this comprehension of life and our place in it, everything that we do on a personal, societal, or planetary level will be fraught with indecision and lack a definitive motivating force. Continual conflict over our philosophies of life divide us and set into motion a "them versus us" mentality.

This treatise may strike many of you as presumptuous. I hope that others will come away more enlightened. For I do realize that the trip on which you are about to embark will challenge your traditional beliefs. But we are at a crossroads in seeing ourselves and everything around us in a new way.

Many futurists and new-agers talk about a paradigm shift. That is exactly what is happening today. Some people cling relentlessly to the old, while others gleefully embrace the changes in order to move forward. My sole purpose is to present this material to you so that you can better grapple with the awesome revolution in thought that we are undergoing at this time in the still very young history of Planet Earth.

William Earl Valentine Key-nee

Chapter 1

Cosmic Origins and History of Humanity

Prior to life of any kind in the vastness of the cosmos, there was nothing. This is a common thread running through folklore and mythology in cultures around the world. A name is given to some supreme being or force that exists in this void that creates everything. That name and its associated title differ from culture to culture. The specific acts it performs, taken literally, may seem unrelated among different peoples. In a philosophical or esoteric perspective, a commonality does pervade all of these ancient stories. (At this initial point in this book, a key understanding has to be established. Words, as a form of communication, lack absolute definition. This means that no two readers always will agree on what is being communicated to them. Take the terms "God" and "infinity." No two individuals will perceive what those terms mean in the same way. On the other hand, if there was no written language with its inherent limitations, and transmission by absolute thought or telepathy was routine, everyone would know exactly what the other person was saying. With this in mind let's proceed.)

Scientists have defined absolute zero as a state of existence in which no motion can occur. Without motion there cannot be physical life, as this requires atoms and molecules vibrating at a certain frequency (or cycles per second). Every cell comprising soil, plants, animals, and people currently exists, in part, because of the rate at which these cells' atoms and molecules are moving. All of the physical matter in the universe is in motion at the microscopic scale.

Energy, too, whether it is light or X-ray radiation, has a vibration. Light travels at the speed of over 186,000 miles per second. X-rays can penetrate solid objects, react with gases, and generate pictures on photographic plates. Another key relationship is that energy and matter are interchangeable, as described in Einstein's equation $E=MC^2$. Here E represents energy, while M stands for the mass of the matter. (Energy is basically the mass of the matter sped up to the speed of light multiplied by itself.)

The idea that neither matter nor energy can be created or destroyed has been accepted universally. This describes a universe in which both matter and energy simply move back and forth from one form to the other. Thus, everything that exists in the cosmos is a part of some larger source that at one time contained all of this energy and matter in a nonmotive condition (absolute zero).

Since cold restricts motion, a warming must have occurred in the source. This source had to exist in a nonphysical state, which some might refer to as "spirit." At that moment when the warming began, motion also started. In another sense it awakened from a cosmic hibernation, resulting in the establishment of energy radiating throughout the universe. Time began as well.

Matter was formed from energy, initially as dust. This was a self-reproductive process comparable to an androgynous, sweat-born procedure. In fact, if the origin of the words "spirit" and "matter" are checked, they refer to father (*pater*) and mother (*mater*), respectively. This principle also led to concepts such as positive/negative, ying/yang, and similar dualities.

But then an even more fantastic event took place. Spirit (energy) and matter interacted and reproduced consciousness as its offspring. Now there exists in the cosmos a self-aware entity with an unlimited mind and the necessary materials from which to build an infinite body. The Big Bang was the mechanism for this construction.

Just as plants, animals, and people must grow from infancy to adulthood, this immense entity (call it The All) similarly has to develop in a parallel manner. It accomplishes this through diverse expressions (stars, planets, and life forms) which, in turn, all grow and experience life at their level of existence. This makes stars and planets "alive" and maturing entities, but at different levels of existence than human.

As human beings live on Planet Earth, so, too, is there life on stars. They are, after all, mature planets. Jupiter, it is said, would have become a star if its evolutionary path had not slowed down during the stabilization of the solar system. This is why, indirectly, sun worshipping (as a form of enlightenment) was practiced by the ancients. This is an innate knowledge that has been "discredited" by modern science. (From where do enlightened beings or wisdom arise?) The infinite diversity of The All manifests itself in countless examples, of which these are a few.

It has been substantiated that from the source came spirit (energy), matter, and consciousness. This leads to seven possible expressions of The All: pure spirit, pure matter, pure consciousness, spirit/matter, spirit/consciousness, matter/consciousness, and spirit/matter/consciousness. Some of these entail physical life forms, while others are invisible to the human eye. Men and women possess the trinity of features mentioned, which is why they have been seen as "born in the image of God." The number seven has a very special place throughout various fields, from religion (the seven churches of Christ) to nature (seven colors of the rainbow) to music (seven musical scales).

The All's seven essential expressions are the basis for everything that exists in the cosmos. In the color spectrum, white represents The All. It is attributed to be the source of total enlightenment. Dividing white produces the seven colors of the rainbow: red, orange, yellow, green, blue, indigo, and violet. This range begins with red at the lower end, then moves to violet at the upper limits of that which human beings can see. Black absorbs all colors of the spectrum (or energies of the cosmos). Similarly, white reflects the complete range (creating energies).

Musical tones are a second related form of sevens that spring forth from The All. Specifically, there are A, B, C, D, E, F, and G within the A-minor scale. Note denominations fall into this pattern as well: sixty-fourth, thirty-second, sixteenth, eighth, quarter, half, and whole. One common term that connects color and music is "tone." (Sixty-four is the number of human DNA essential components.)

Energy forms present a third aspect resembling these expressions. At the weak side of the frequency spectrum, there are atmospheric (earth) waves. They are followed by radio waves, microwaves (radar), visible light, ultrasound, and gamma rays moving toward the stronger end. Amazingly, there is a direct relationship between these frequencies and the seven senses of life: touch, taste, smell, sight, hearing, intuition, and thought-transference.

Chakras, or human physical energy centers, have particular vibratory manifestations attuned to these varying frequencies. The coccygeal chakra represents the base for physical survival. Ability to feel others' emotions is performed by the sacral chakra. In the solar plexus the psychic capabilities are distributed throughout the body. The throat chakra is the center for communication. Psychic abilities are performed via the spiritual or third eye. Finally, capping the body's chakras is the crown, home for pure intuition and knowingness.

Finally, there are added correlations between these individual fields of study and the evolutionary process. Some refer to them as kingdoms: mineral, plant, animal, human, etheric, astral, and causal. The mineral world is composed strictly of matter. Next, the plant kingdom represents matter and energy. (Scientific studies reveal that trees, for example, do possess electricity. They even "scream" or emit waves when thirsty, which insects pick up, resulting in infestation.)

Matter and consciousness combine to form the animal world. Investigations of various species demonstrate their self-awareness to a limited degree. Humanity, as mentioned, is a physical expression of matter/spirit/consciousness. A few individuals from the metaphysical community state that the human family is at the point of co-creation with The All, exhibited by the explosion of the atom bomb (that splits atoms).

Further along the developmental route are three additional states of existence. One is the etheric realm, where psychic abilities are a major aspect of semiphysical beings composed of energy and consciousness. From here there is the astral world of total invisibility or pure energy. At the reigning pinnacle one finds the causal realm of pure consciousness. ("Causal" means causing something to happen.)

All of the seven concepts are intermeshed throughout the cosmos. From the lowly mineral (red, sixty-fourth, C, touch, coccygeal chakra, atmospheric waves) level to the causal (violet, whole, B, thought transference, crown chakra, gamma rays) point of the scale, the interconnection of this world and the infinite are one.

A DNA/note denomination link was noted previously. The DNA provides the instructions for cell formation that constructs people, animals, and so forth. This, in turn, is related directly to the sixty-four hexagrams of the I Ching, an ancient Chinese method for divination or revealing hidden truths. A discovery of a one-to-one equation of the hexagrams to the DNA code was found when written in a binary order. This binary code underlies all genetic, electrical, electromagnetic, and neurological functions.

A trinary relationship also has been shown to comprise The All. Energy/matter/consciousness are expressed in the three basic colors: red, green, and blue. People releasing their hot tempers are said to be seeing red, an emotional act. The physical world of matter shows its springtime rebirth through a greening of the land. Dark blue or purple was the color of royalty and the priesthood, reflecting wisdom or higher consciousness.

Brain wavelengths are connected to this discussion. Beta waves describe the initial frequencies derived from the alpha/omega (beginning/end), exhibiting the creative energies of thought.

The dream state of theta waves stands for the manifestation of energy. Then there is the higher state of consciousness at the delta level.

In addition to these acknowledgements, a few more should be declared. Chemistry is the study of the interaction of energy and matter. Mind/brain investigators are delving into the concerns related to matter and consciousness linkages. Consciousness and energy are the purview of those mind researchers in the neurosciences and parapsychology. Cosmology encompasses the entirety of matter/energy/consciousness as it fits together in all of its massive complexity. As one breaks down chemistry into its triune characteristics, light interacts with matter at high temperatures over long time frames. Heat and matter do the same but at low energies in short intervals of time. Sound and matter come down somewhere in between both of these in energy range and time periods.

This presents an awesome picture of cosmic proportions. Life is indeed extremely complex. These small number of examples demonstrate that the narrow fields of study that Western science has subdivided into disclose that there is something being lost in how the world is currently understood to work.

The terminology used in detailing the cosmic puzzle leads to disagreement among all the different professionals trying to comprehend its enormity. This proves that they all are describing the same essential aspects of The All.

Before going on to probe the human side of the story, the growth of the human birth womb must be examined. Planet Earth may seem unintelligible, but the basics of its development can be embraced easily.

The Earth's Formation

The Earth began as have (and will) all planets. Dust particles stuck together after colliding and cooling. This driving energy maintained a spinning action that held the particles in an increasing compact body. As the material grew, meteors struck and remained part of it. The extremely hot center failed to cool; its outer skin did.

Impacts trickled off approximately 4.45 billion years ago. For all practical purposes they ceased about 3.9 billion years ago. By this time the crust had formed, although it was thin. RNA and DNA arrived on the scene some 400 million years later. Inanimate matter then transcended into bacteria 100 million years after that. Sunlight provided a stimulus for sugar fermentation, which boosted the electrons of the microorganisms to higher energy states.

Every nook of the Earth was teeming with bacteria at around 2.5 billion years ago. Ultraviolet radiation initiated sexual reproduction, which assisted many life forms in amplifying their useful inventions (photosynthesis, genetic engineering, embryo development, and so on). The environment, however, was totally alien to anyone who could travel back in time. All cells lacked nuclei and grew without oxygen, but created the fundamental ecosystem that has led to that of today.

Approximately 2 billion years ago, there was an unprecedented holocaust of life. This was, perhaps, the first planetary pollution crisis. It immersed the globe and all of its residents in oxygen. DNA continued to replicate. Genes were transferred. Mutations ran rampant. Unknown numbers of life forms disappeared, while new superorganisms called "the microcosm" came onto the scene. Cells possessing nuclei also started to appear, all with the ability to use oxygen. It was a jump in evolution comparable to a leap from the era of Kitty

Hawk directly to the age of the Concorde.

The duality that fills life at every level became apparent during this time period. Cells either did or didn't have nuclei. There was nothing in between. The jump in the evolution of organisms was one not instituted by mutation or the transfer of genes. It was defined as a symbiosis, a sudden blending of independent forms of life into something larger than itself. (This is why there are missing links.) In this case plants were the result of a coming together of algae and fungi.

Seven hundred million years ago the first sea creatures were swimming around in the seventy percent of the planet's environment. Then 300 million years later, jawed fish came ashore. Mammals appeared around 125 million years ago, laying their eggs. Flowers also were part of the scenery. An interesting note: the human brain and central nervous system evolved as an adaptation for eating plants and plant consumers. Plants do not need such sophisticated mechanisms since their genes activate the chemistry of their bodies.

Land dwellers require a varied muscle arrangement and a hardier bone structure than those living in water. Lungs also change due to increased amounts of oxygen that they must process. Skin and surface coatings are necessary to deal with the harsh and unfiltered light that is prevalent. The movement out of the liquid surroundings was thrust upon those creatures by geological upheaval, one of many periodic events.

These catastrophes have been the driving forces behind major (and minor) alterations in the development of the planet. The anaerobic bacteria, so dependent upon hydrogen for their existence, died out in huge numbers when the Earth's magnetic field shifted. Photosynthesis became a process that used water for assimilating nutrients. The oxygen crisis had killed off these initial life forms in droves about 1 billion years ago.

During this time frame, new bacteria that used oxygen were the innovators. They applied bio-chemical energy more efficiently. These unique microbes were the beginning stage for increasingly complex organisms that symbiotically were trans-formed into plants, animals, and people. But it took an unprecedented event 245 million years back in early prehistory--a meteoric impact--that brought about the mammals.

Evidence of a similar although less powerful strike occurred approximately 66 million years ago. This was the age of dinosaurs. They were destroyed en mass when an extraterrestrial boul-der hit the planet's surface (in present day Iowa) throwing up tremendous amounts of dust into the atmosphere. This blocked out the sun's rays and plunged the world into an ice age. On the other hand, it cleared the way for primates and the associated hand-eye coordination that led to the development of technology.

Supercontinents

The era of the dinosaur was also the last appear-ance of a supercontinent. These continental bodies were combinations of most or all land masses that existed throughout the planet's developmental process. The first formed about 2.8 billion years ago and was named Kenora. It was part Africa and North America.

A second supercontinent, Amazonia, came together around 1.5 billion years ago. This was a uniting of Kenora and Australia. Baikalia exhibited major portions of eastern Asia, plus many south-ern continents, 700 million years later. Next, Gondwanaland included India, Africa, Arabia,

South America, Antarctica, plus southern Australia about 300 million years after that. Pangaea, consisting of all of today's continental masses, united approximately 220 million years ago and was the home of the dinosaurs. (Skeletal remains have been found on all continents.)

Root Races of Man

One of the direct descendants of humanity lived at that time as well. The seven possible expressions of The All again relate to men and women as well as all life forms. Thus, there are seven root races of the human species. There is nothing known about the first two root races, as they were as distinct in their appearance to human beings as an adult is to a fetus in the womb.

The third root race, however, has been mentioned in myth and matches much of the biologic evolution of life overall. They inhabited this last supercontinent, which has been referred to in folklore as Lemuria. In the story of Ulysses and the cyclops, the one-eyed creature that he battles is that descendant. Fish and animals existing at this time had a single optical instrument that eventually recessed into the brain, forming the pineal gland.

Lemuria and the Garden of Eden

Physical stature was the prevalent characteristic of life at that time. The Lemurian cyclops was fifty to sixty feet tall. Its skin was tougher than that of an elephant. Colorings ranged from black to brown to red. Reproduction resulted from a process known as sweat-born, where the ova is released from the pores and fertilized outside of the body. This, too, reflects many other forms of life prior to and during this period. At a later point in its evolution, the Lemurian did lay eggs. The senses of this being were extremely dull, as the environment produced noxious fumes and living conditions that the men and women of today could not possibly tolerate.

Before Lemuria or Pangaea split apart, a visitation of sorts took place. It was a spectacular event, in that beings arrived via light (not a spaceship). Just as in the story of Jonathan Livingston Seagull, Jonathan is told that he can travel solely by thinking about a destination. These entities had that capability. A few masters and other spiritually dedicated individuals throughout history have demonstrated this ability.

The purpose of this journey was to protect a certain elite of the Lemurian race who would be taught to think and be taught the practice of hatha yoga. This latter ritual helped with posture-related physical prowess. The nurturing and training was completed on what has been dubbed the Sacred White Island, where they were taken before the continent was destroyed.

The ultimate force tearing this supercontinent apart and eliminating the dinosaurs and most Lemurians was the impact of a meteor about 66 million years ago. The impact caused an immense dust cloud to rise in the atmosphere that blocked out the precious sunlight necessary for survival of those species. An additional change that came out of this event was a mutation of genes. The first man and woman (Adam and Lilith) eventually were produced from these transformations. They lacked the self-awareness that is currently taken for granted by modern people.

The tale of the Garden of Eden relates a point in their evolution at which they gained that perspective of self. The Tree of Knowledge stood for this concept. Eating the apple represented a transcendence from holistic awareness (connection to all life) to self-awareness (at which the ego takes hold). It also demonstrated a progression from Lemurian or physical emphasis to emotional accentuation. (Ego must be part of the makeup of the personality for emotions to be expressed. Spiritual masters have shown this to be true.)

Myths from elsewhere center on such symbology in regard to self-realization. This is shadowed in pictures of gardens containing trees and a fruit that possesses hidden knowledge. But it is truly a representation of the advancement of the species that takes place following some jolt in planetary functions from an outside or extraterrestrial source, including meteors and comets. But life is extremely complicated and there are unique beings who have yet to reveal themselves to most of the people inhabiting Planet Earth.

Geology provides evidence of all of these occurrences according to the timetable previously outlined. No paleontological findings have uncovered cyclops-like creatures fitting this description. But if the impact was so severe, many bodies no doubt were incinerated while others sank below the ocean depths and dissolved. Conversely, information has surfaced with regard to Atlantis.

Atlantis

There have been numerous indications throughout the Atlantic and Mediterranean waters that show evidence of lands that once were above sea level. Discoveries of building structures and human artifacts have been uncovered in photographs from undersea investigations in these vicinities. It is known that South America and Africa were connected, as were North America and Europe, during Pangaean times. As it broke apart, all four of these land masses allowed Atlantic Ocean formation. Some mountains also stood above these waters.

Plato's writings provide the basis for information about Atlantis. He reports in the Dialogues that it was a kind of paradise. It was said to consist of magnificent mountain ranges, lush plains teeming with a large variety of animals, and luxurious gardens of abundant fruits. The land was rich with precious metals, especially the revered iridescent orchalc (a copper alloy that may have been brass).

Atlantis, according to Plato, was an island greater in size than Libya and Asia combined. Its capital, constructed in the center, had buildings of white, black, and red stone blended harmoniously together in wondrous splendor. The arrangement of the city was such that it consisted of five zones laid out in perfect concentric circles. Numerous ports were available and served the inner areas through a system of canals. Ships from various locales harbored there and made it a very busy place of business.

A great palace and temple existed at the heart of the city. Silver and gold architecture laced nearly all of the outer facades. Inner ceilings and walls were covered with ivory, orchalc, gold, and silver. Statues of gold, including the god Poseidon standing in a chariot that touched the roof, made a truly awe-inspiring sight. Ten rulers of the island, although rich and powerful, governed with wisdom over their colonial empires. The laws of Poseidon sat in plain view in front of his image in the temple, inscribed on a stone pillar. Peace and justice reigned due to the universality of the legal code.

In the end Atlantean society decayed as the pursuit of material wealth and idleness became their false gods. Plato attributed this to the fact that the divine aspect of humanity too often is diluted by human nature. A war of world conquest followed. Huge fleets of ships set sail against settlements along the Mediterranean. Only the Athenians, with their goddess Athena (wisdom, industry, war), proved to be a match for the Atlanteans, and won a brilliant victory.

Finally, the gods destroyed Atlantis through violent earthquakes and floods. Plato said that it disappeared beneath the waters in a single day about 12,000 years ago. He situated the island beyond the Pillars of Hercules (Straits of Gibraltar) in the Great Ocean or Western Sea. (Indian poetry from the Mahabharata and Ramayana contain similar versions of the placement of this civilization.)

Another source for this story came from the ancient Egyptians. Solon, one of the Seven Sages of Greece, told Plato that he had learned of Atlantis from the priests of the goddess Neith. On his trip made six centuries before Christ, these highly educated men told Solon about antiquated historical records they possessed. One priest recounted the heroic deeds of his Athenean ancestors and the tragedy of Atlantis. The Egyptians, who were meticulous record-keepers of the past, seem to be the preservers of this long-dead civilization on their stone tablets and in sacred archives. They also indicate Egyptian contacts through trade.

Psychic Edgar Cayce complemented this general description. Those who knew him say he never read Plato's Dialogues. Cayce, while in a trance, related that Atlantis had a high level of material and spiritual standards. They were knowledgeable in the principles of flight. Cayce saw the end of Atlantis occurring at the same time as Plato had and explained that the rulers had misused their knowledge. He spots its location as somewhere between the Gulf of Mexico and the Straits of Gibraltar. As an added bit of information, Cayce stated that the inhabitants knew that Atlantis would be destroyed in advance, permitting many to move to other areas of the world (Egypt, the Americas).

Investigators point to the Azores, Bimini, or Santorini (Crete) as the primary possible sites for Atlantis. It is known that volcanic activity has produced islands (Hawaii, Japan, and others). In 1963 the birth of a new isle south of Iceland in the Atlantic was observed, and the isle was named Surtsey. By late 1965 it had grown to 550 feet in height, one-and-a-third miles in length, and a square mile in area. (It continued to enlarge for two more years.)

During the laying of the first trans-Atlantic cable between North America and Europe in the 1860s, a group of mountain ranges was discovered running north and south under the Atlantic Ocean. Upon taking core samples from deep within these submerged mountains, two distinctive findings were recorded. First, they had a history of volcanic activity. Second, about 12,000 years ago the lava had dried above sea level.

American zoologist Dr. Manson Valentine amplified this data with his discovery of strange structures under the waters off the coast of Bimini in 1958. They were curious in that they exhibited regular polygons, circles, triangles, rectangles, and dead straight lines extending for several miles. In 1968 he and a group of divers found a giant wall hundreds of yards long submerged north of the island. Two branches of the wall were constructed at right angles, in precise perpendicularity. The building blocks of the structure consisted of massive stones over sixteen feet square. As further exploration took place, a huge harbor complex was observed with quays and a double jetty.

Studies surrounding these discoveries have

shown that a portion of Bimini subsided over 10,000 years ago as the sea level rose, the result of the melting of polar glaciers. The undersea finds have been determined to be artificial and of a fairly distant period. Adding to all of this data is the fact that Edgar Cayce predicted Atlantis would be resurrected in 1968 or 1969 from the silt and waves of the ocean.

The Lake of Seven Cities is an old volcanic crater in the Azores. It is a favorite site for those hunting for Atlantis. They postulate that beneath the ash and debris on the bottom of the crater is the Atlantean capital of Poseidopolis.

Santorini also fits this description. It is a flooded crater stretching a total of 32 miles. Soaring cliffs almost 1,000 feet high mark its rim and then plunge 1,300 feet to the depths of the waters. Santorini now looks like a string of islands that can conform to the canal layout contained in Plato's Dialogues.

Atlantis was the equivalent of the first human civilization. Stones were the basic technology of early primates, while crystals were their highest form. If one stops to consider this in terms of folklore, there is some truth to the stories told about it. Crystals *are* the highest form of stones. Crystal skulls or other shaped rocks do have some unique properties as demonstrated by science. Whether early societies had powerful technologies comparable to what has been built today (or totally different) is not inconceivable. The minds of men and women have not changed in their capabilities, as studies of the past have revealed.

As previously mentioned, Atlantis contained the initial remnants of the human family. The normal two eyes were a common mutation that characterized many life forms, with that center eye receding into the brain to become the pineal gland.

Not much is known about the function of this or any other part of the most-complicated organ, when compared to all other body parts. But more is being uncovered as the years proceed.

The peoples of Atlantis were black, brown, and yellow. Emotions were the predominant attribute of this root race, and still remain a potent trait. It also proved to be the downfall of this civilization. The tale of Sodom and Gomorrah relates that the emotional nature of the inhabitants became so strong that they lost control. The result was the flood that has been recorded in the geologic records. It was not a supernatural event--the sea level began returning to previous heights 12,000 years after another meteoric impact and magnetic reversal had occurred.

Before this catastrophe struck, the visitors returned. This "Spiritual Hierarchy," as metaphysicians have called them, chose another group of people to nurture and prepare for the great change. Many of them scattered to various locales: China, India, Europe, Egypt, and the Americas. The select ones became the priests and shamans of these cultures. As the water rose, the small island of Poseidon remained. This was completely destroyed around 13,000 B.C. as stated by a number of channels, and can be confirmed by evidence already mentioned. The similarities in culture the world over, such as architecture and folklore, are explained by this as well.

Semitic/Caucasian Revelations

Caucasians are the most recent members of the human family. The species has gone through several genetic changes that affected the evolution of humanity. In fact, the colors of the rainbow reflect the development of physical life forms on Planet

Earth. Stars, like people, proceed (in reverse) from white to violet to yellow to red to black throughout their lives. Everything is interwoven within the cosmic picture.

Originally, the Semitic peoples came onto the scene with the ancient Babylonians, Assyrians, Arameans, Phoenicians, and others. This race appears in the archaeological record in succession of the Atlantean catastrophe. They are made up of more than just the Jewish ethnicity, including the Arabian peoples. Within their communities they became the initiators of two keys to the advancement of humanity.

Science has established that previous human beings did not have the ability to physically assimilate milk products beyond childhood. It was a genetic mutation in the DNA that led to this previously unincorporated factor in human physiology. The first nomadic tribes began to herd dairy cattle during this period. (Of course, this wandering came about after leaving Atlantis.)

The protein content of milk and associated dairy products is known to be the most concentrated form (of protein) available to men and women. It proved to add much to the physical and mental accomplishments of these peoples. Among those successes was the establishment of a written means of communication, starting with a system of symbols. This expanded with time into language.

Record keeping began with the origination of tokens that evolved into writing. Prior to this, history was seen as restarting with each new generation. Due to the fact that the skills of society before this epoch were hunting, fishing, and simple agriculture, there was no real need for history to be kept.

Counting, as a vehicle for documenting what belonged to whom, took thousands of years to

develop. Clay tokens that were used between 10,000
B.C. and 6000 B.C. by Sumerian and Mesopotamian
civilizations were first dug up in the Middle East.
Numerals have been uncovered dating back to
around 3000 B.C. They appeared on pictographic
tablets, next in cuneiform notation, and then as
Aramaic script. This spread from Babylonia to
Greece, where Pythagoras, Euclid, and others
applied it to the foundation of mathematics.

This details another leap in the understanding
and development of the species. When seen as one
of the "Chosen People," an insight can be made
here. Metaphysicians claim that the planet goes
through a series of ages reflecting astrological
signs and star groups. Interestingly, there are
correlations between the ages and what was happening at that time in the past. Science also has
shown connections between sunspot activity,
weather conditions, and human circumstances
over periods of time (see Chapter 4).

Astro-Historical Linkages

The era before 6000 B.C. was highlighted by a
civilization in the southwestern area of Asia. It
exhibited characteristics of equality between genders, although women were considered of primary
importance due to their association with fertility.
This was the Age of Gemini, where twins (as studies
have shown) possessed equality of abilities, feelings, thoughts, and physical appearance. Its prominent concept was thinking, as demonstrated by the
peaceful, cooperative civilization that existed.

It is said that Abraham's father was an idol-
maker. He lived during the Age of Taurus. Possessions and idols were a major part of the artifacts
uncovered between 4000 and 6000 B.C. They also
go with this astrological epoch. The golden calf was

worshipped. Krishna established the Hindu religion with the cow as a sacred animal. "I have" is the accompanying ideal that directly relates to this Taurine era.

Four thousand years ago Moses was in contact with the Spiritual Hierarchy. He escaped death as an infant and was educated by the Egyptian nobility. His famous encounter with the burning bush is an expression of communicating with that hierarchy. The New Covenant represented the choosing of a new tribe to progress another rung on the evolutionary ladder. This Age of Aries, the ram, was one of self. Moses requested a name to give to the people as provider of the commandments. The response was "I Am That I Am." It also was an era of sheep sacrifices, the ram's horn, and King David's flock.

Then at the break in the time scale, the Lamb of God appeared on the scene. This ushered in the Age of Pisces. Within this epoch there was the rise of a new belief system that was incorporated into various institutions. Yet the other religions still persist today. The "water into wine" and "fisher of men" ideas all correspond to Pisces (the fish). The seas have been conquered (at least the surface), which goes hand-in-hand with this age. Associated sayings and terms that exemplify the Piscean "I believe" ideal are "Give me that old time religion"; "Yours to do or die"; and God-fearing Christian."

In the 1960s there was much talk about the Age of Aquarius. Free love, peace, and the release of creative energies filled the planet. The brotherhood of man theme commonly was expounded by many people. The initial stages of that era began with the first flight, the blimp voyage into the air above Paris in 1898. Aquarius is indeed an air sign! But it alludes to much more. The journey into mind sciences and an urge to really know God have launched a New Age movement.

An examination of this movement will commence in Chapter 2. The key to comprehending it must be preceded by an in-depth look at the twentieth century, for it is in unraveling this moment in time that the not-so-distant past and the immediate future can add to that understanding.

Religio-Historical Implications

In the 1900s a civilization wrought with religious and political differences has seen its share of violent disagreement between citizens and countries. This is due to the evident continuity of history. The tribal chief and shaman were looked upon by the members as ones who could communicate with God or the spirit world. The king and queen figures followed, as God's earthly representatives possessing "pure blood." These individuals or families maintained good relations with a specific religious order which, in turn, gave its blessings to the royal family. Schooling of the privileged was performed by the priests-scientists of the day. Out of the "I know best for the rest" philosophy came the dictator.

The next system manifesting itself was rule by a group of elites. Numerous qualifications were established for holding office (property owner, educational credentials, ability to raise sufficient funds for the campaign, and so forth). The style of obtaining a position varied from nation to nation (elections by minority, majority, or plurality; appointment by other government officials; and so on). Religious involvement in state-run operations gave way to secular influences.

Science, too, separated from religion during this transition from kingship to rule by a group elite. Stilted, dogmatic beliefs were being propagated by the priests, who resisted questioning and hushed opposition. Science provided an outlet for inquiry about life. Its premise, truth seeking, established a framework for universal state education. That led to the revolutions that took place all over the world and continued into the twentieth century. They began with the American Revolution. As a result of the formation of the United States, minimal oversight of citizen activities was instituted. Individual actions were to be guided by the freedom to apply personal religious convictions. Conversely, the Union of Soviet Socialist Republics came about with an emphasis on science as the director for conduct in the advancement of the human family in a collective orientation. Other variations of these two systems have been tried in other countries.

Both of these governmental forms evolved from the original superstitious and then religious practices of a single representative of God who was the all-knowing head of society. As the teachings became rigid, dogmatic beliefs that were interpreted differently by numerous sects of that same religion (diversity incarnate), the right-versus-wrong argument entered the picture. Now governments exhibit that same mentality. International disagreements arose from religious and political philosophies professing one true way to structure and operate societies.

Twentieth-Century Insight

As populations grew and technologies advanced, great wars were predicted by the science fiction writers of the late nineteenth century. Both Verne and Wells, among others, presented this negative perspective of the future. They grasped the driving forces that pervaded that period of history.

Military technologies and man's egotism, with prominent mind-sets of narrow beliefs, were a devastating combination. Whether it was the thought of reuniting peoples under one flag or the creation of the "perfect" society, the conflict arrived because of a misunderstanding about how the evolution of global civilization takes shape.

World War II demonstrated this thinking with overwhelming results. Hitler's twisted view of the previous material, mixed with his personal eccentricities, were essential to the outcome. But there were, in addition to this, weak or ignorant leaders around the world who failed to stand up to the bully of Germany. The Führer was supported greatly by the energies and thoughts from his own country's citizens. These and other elements produced an environment for war.

It took strong political chiefs to combine their resources in order to defeat Germany and Japan. This was much like a minor illness that is left to fester until it becomes so devastating that it takes a powerful treatment to cure it. In the case of the war, it took the production and application of the atomic bomb. This device, or something similar, was the only solution to halt the power unleashed by the German nation and its allies.

The explosion of the atomic bombs that ended the war was a tremendous signal transmitted through the corridors of the universe. It attracted the attention of neighbors residing in other parts of the cosmos. Then, in 1947, the first visiting vehicle from another planet was spotted by Ken Arnold in the United States. Coincidentally, at this period in history, the last group of Chosen People were returning to what they considered their homeland.

Following the First World War, the League of Nations was formed in an attempt to prevent any further global conflict. It was an organization out of time and place. The countries of this planet were not yet ready for such a mechanism. It took the unprecedented release of energies and the associated awareness of their impact to stimulate a formation of the United Nations. This very crucial forum is in its infancy and will increase its diplomatic abilities as the people of the Earth mature.

After World War II was resolved, the United States opened its national wallet to assist in rebuilding Europe and Japan. Missed opportunities and misunderstandings led to the Cold War. During the 1950s the young nations who had been dominated (as some parents wish to keep control of their kids) started questioning their rulers and yearning for independence. The 1960s brought forth both personal and national actions to break free of old ways that had been too restrictive.

Rebellion, whether by children or peoples being governed, should indicate that a flexibility must be instituted to allow for further growth and expansion. Drug use began as such a vehicle. As with all experimentation, there will be some who become abusers or addicts, while others make unknown discoveries about themselves and life itself. All of this added increasingly to the chaos and disorder of the times.

With the election of John Kennedy, a new generation looked toward the future with extreme optimism in the United States. The Peace Corps was established to render development assistance in the Third World on a personal, one-to-one basis. Yet America's own underprivileged struck out for their rights and opportunities. Riots started tearing apart the South.

Kennedy was assassinated in Dallas due to three main groups holding him in contempt (and fearing a mythical family dynasty as a real possibility). Black protests and administration responses threatened the status quo in cultural traditions, business operations, and among white separatists. Organized crime was faced with a minimum of eight years of legal pressure by Attorney General Robert Kennedy. Intelligence forces became Kennedy's personal target after the Bay of Pigs fiasco. These disruptions of everyday life were the keys to his death. (His alleged assassin also was murdered shortly thereafter.)

As the black social movement coalesced into a cohesive crusade behind Martin Luther King, Jr., riots spread to the North. Malcolm X was shot and killed. The white supremacists firmed up support and went on the rampage. Watts (California) exploded, leading to major property damage and some deaths. A Black Power conference was held.

Out of the civil rights drive, antiwar dissidents called for an end to U.S. involvement in Vietnam. Dr. King led a peaceful march in New York; another took place in San Francisco. Riots continued among blacks in the central United States. King later was killed in Memphis. The act was followed closely by Robert Kennedy's shooting in California during the presidential campaign.

Meanwhile, American troop casualties escalated in Vietnam. The bloody Chicago tumult ensued in the streets outside the Democratic convention. Crimes of violence, accordingly, rose over 50 percent nationwide. Charles Manson and his "family" were tried for the murder of actress Sharon Tate and her friends. Even a Boston strangler came onto the scene.

Around the world in the 1960s similar events were in progress. Apartheid was condemned by the United Nations. The Berlin Wall was constructed. U.N. Representative Dag Hammarskjöld died in flight on his way to an African conference. The Cuban missile crisis threatened to cause World

War III. A Buddhist-led military coup took place in South Vietnam. Turkey and Cyprus came into conflict over Greece's abrogation of a trilateral treaty. Khrushchev was replaced as Prime Minister of Russia.

Rounding out the decade, the violence swelled. An Algerian revolution occurred. International protests declared U.S. policy in Vietnam to be improper. Students rebelled in Madrid, London, and Paris. The Chinese Red Guard demonstrated against Western influences taking hold in their country. There was a military coup in Ghana. A six-day war between the Arabs and Israelis grew out of earlier skirmishes. Uprisings in Warsaw over cultural restrictions led to a Soviet invasion. Violent fighting broke out in Northern Ireland, causing British troops to enter the fray to curb civil war.

Natural disasters struck globally, one after the other. Earthquakes rocked Iran, Yugoslavia, Alaska, and Chile. Unusually heavy rains plus flooding hit northern Italy, eastern Brazil, and California. Hurricanes, tornadoes, and cyclones inundated eastern Pakistan, Cuba, Haiti, the Midwest of the U.S., as well as the Mississippi gulf coast. An electrical outage paralyzed the northeastern part of the United States and southeastern Canada. An ocean pollution conference in Rome drew 39 representatives of interested nations.

Music and the more creative outlets manifested innovative ideas during the 1960s. Folk singers Joan Baez, Bob Dylan, and others added their voices to the foray through their songs. "Born Free," "Ballad of the Green Berets," and "Stoned Soul Picnic" celebrated themes of the decade. The Woodstock Music and Art Fair brought 300,000 people to a New York farm.

Television and film took Americans into the "Outer Limits" and "The Twilight Zone." The phenomenon of "Star Trek" began a shaky three-year excursion into the great unknown, later to take off in syndicated reruns. Movies including *Dr. Strangelove, Help, Fahrenheit 451, In the Heat of the Night, 2001: A Space Odyssey,* and *Easy Rider* reflected the times.

In the realm of science America launched into space in an attempt to keep up with Russia. President Kennedy established a space program with the goal of reaching the Moon by 1969 (which was met). Underwater circumnavigation of the globe was completed by a U.S. submarine. Atomic energy lit up America, Britain, and the U.S.S.R.

Medicine conceived and began using the artificial heart, plastic arteries, and valve replacements. The initial heart transplants were performed. Additives and DDT were discovered to be cancer-causing agents. Thalidomide babies were born, disrupting the normal genetic codes. *Silent Spring* was written by Rachel Carson, setting the stage for legislation to control pollution and raising environmental awareness.

The 1970s

Turbulence intensified as the 1970s took shape. The Weathermen underground initiated terrorist activities in the United States. A National Guard unit killed four students at Kent University in Ohio. The war in Vietnam expanded into Laos and Cambodia. Arthur Bremer shot Alabama Governor George Wallace, paralyzing him for life. Two assassination attempts were made on Gerald Ford, who replaced Richard Nixon.

Nixon, of course, was forced to resign as the Watergate investigation revealed his knowledge of the affair. This was the first incident of its kind in American history, which set a sinister precedent.

The president's law-and-order stance demonstrated his sincere concern about society getting out of control. A wage, profits, and price freeze was indicative of the drastic steps taken by Nixon.

The Ford and Carter terms were faced with huge increases in oil costs as a group of Arab countries made a start at controlling their own lives. An "energy catastrophe" and the "moral equivalent of war" were invoked as expressions to describe the extent of the situation. The typical American's reaction was the same as a child who had his or her candy taken away.

Additional financial crises were an important part of this decade. New York City approached default. It was saved by Congress. Rapid rises in malpractice insurance and long hours provoked a work slowdown and strikes by doctors around the U.S. The lengthiest miners' work stoppage also took place in the States. A plunge in the dollar caused it to fall to record lows. Major daily papers were closed for months by labor negotiations on both sides of the Atlantic.

Domestically, the chaos swelled to a fever pitch. Twenty bodies were found in a rural California field. A five-day uprising by prisoners occurred in Attica, New York. Hijacking became a serious problem for air travelers. Heiress Patricia Hearst was kidnapped and apparently joined her captors, proving no one is safe or above brainwashing. Streaking, running nude in public, became the latest craze. Legionnaire's disease, a mysterious illness, struck or killed 200 people attending a convention in Philadelphia. David Berkowitz, driven by a voice from his dog, made headlines as the "Son of Sam" killer. Women were admitted to the Air Force Academy. Militant American Indians occupied Wounded Knee, South Dakota, for seventy days. Gay rights movements took hold.

These tragic and novel incidents merely indicate what was going on all over the world. King Hussein escaped assassination in Jordan. The same thing happened in the Philippines during the visit of Pope Paul IV. Britain imposed direct rule upon Northern Ireland after years of bloody battles, resulting in an importation of some of the violence. Terrorists murdered Israeli athletes at the Munich Olympics while similar activities were carried out in Italy, Argentina, and West Germany. The culmination of these acts saw American hostages taken during the Iranian revolution.

India and Pakistan went to war. Ferdinand Marcos instituted martial law as the Philippines were threatened by civil war. Arabs and Israelis clashed once again. Chile's elected government was overthrown by a military junta. An Ethiopian internal rift split the country. Christians and Moslems began a confrontation in Lebanon that literally tore it apart. Blacks in South Africa battled armed police in an attempt to eliminate apartheid.

Nicaraguan and Angolan internal conflicts added to the increasing global strife that symbolized the growth pains on Planet Earth.

Storms and other calamities continued to propagate. Cyclones and floods struck East Pakistan. A tidal wave, generated by a cyclone, inundated Bengal. Hurricanes Agnes and Belle caused much damage to the eastern United States. Bangladesh underwent another flood. Mauna Loa, a volcano in Hawaii, erupted for the first time in 25 years. Later on, volcanic potency was unleashed in Hawaii as well as Japan and Italy. Two million were made homeless by a third cyclone hitting India and typhoons disrupting Taiwan and the Philippines.

Earthquakes were rampant in this period. Every part of the planet except Australia and Canada felt the effects of the moving substructure. Los Angeles, Nicaragua, Guatemala, Argentina, and Mexico experienced much damage in the Americas. Elsewhere, Burma's Temples of the Pagan were demolished. Italy, China, Turkey, Bali, the Philippines, Greece, Japan, and Iran went through similar devastation.

Deadly accidents proliferated. An historic London subway crash killed or injured nearly 150 people. Downed airplanes produced huge amounts of casualties in Turkey, Yugoslavia, the Canary Islands, and New York. In a replay of the 1960s, New York City suffered an extensive power blackout. Looting, vandalism, and fires resulted this time around. Oil tankers ran ashore or broke apart on both shores of the Atlantic Ocean, spilling hundreds of thousands of tons of the black gold. U.S. Representative Leo Ryan was among those murdered in Guyana by members of Jim Jones' Peoples Temple. A massive suicide followed.

Film mirrored this conscious awakening. *Catch 22, A Clockwork Orange, The Conformist, Frenzy, One Flew Over the Cuckoo's Nest, All the President's Men,* and *Network* were some of the most popular of that medium. Many won awards for their composition. "Roots" was another acclaimed television miniseries. But as they say, the arts reflected society.

Scientific spectaculars filled the world of news. On the heels of several Moon landings, Skylab was placed in orbit as the United States prolonged its string of achievements. Within a few years the Space Shuttle was launched. A man sued the U.S. government and won after having his skin altered from black to white. India joined the nuclear weapons club when it exploded a bomb. Chlorofluorocarbons were discovered to have properties capable of eating away the Earth's ozone layer. The first test tube baby was born in England. Smaller and smaller particles in the cosmos were observed by physicists.

The 1980s

Entering a new decade always seems like a fresh start. With the election of Ronald Reagan, who made America feel good about itself through his exuberant praise of the citizenry, things appeared to be changing for the better. But, alas, he was only human. As his term ended it was obvious that the public had moved away from his agenda, although they clearly liked the man.

The drug issue exploded. Cocaine took on social prominence as the "in" substance to use. Comedian Richard Pryor almost burnt himself to death during a smoking binge. Actor John Belushi overdosed on it. Even a millionaire car manufacturer (John DeLorean) was convicted for trafficking in it.

The Caribbean, South America, and the Gulf Coast of the United States became the triangle of production, smuggling, and laundering arenas for the drug of choice. In the islands, Colombia, and other neighboring countries, powerful kingpins transformed themselves from crooks into employers as well as benefics for the poor. Government corruption, along with the armies of the drug lords, succeeded in preventing extraditions or legal challenges to their interests.

In the United States bankers, law enforcement officials, and celebrities all have been touched by the immense amounts of money that is a part of these operations. Miami, Florida, surpassed the city of Chicago (in Prohibition days) as the most tainted police department in the country. The monetary rewards also trickled down to the ghettos, where gangs fighting over their "territories" sent murder rates and violence out of sight.

With tax revenues dropping and the revolt of the late 1970s still fresh in the minds of politicians, legalized gambling was seen as one additional vehicle to get the citizens to willingly cough up their money. Lotteries were established in state after state. However, as the tax rates on income have proven to be hardest on the poor, so, too, has the lottery system. (A 1988 Florida study revealed that three of the least prosperous counties provided the greatest percentage of revenue from those least able to play it.)

Business was rocked by a stock market crash in 1987. This era has been beset with its share of financial scandal. Insider trading led to the conviction of wealthy individuals who could either not get enough or were caught up in the game of stock trading. A few congressmen fell into criminal activities when helping those in the private sector to defraud the government. Still others insured that their multibillion dollar companies would secure huge, enriching contracts with the military.

Reagan's administration also had problems. As his last year came to a close, there was much debate about the federal deficit. Talk centered on how much the government borrowed to pay its bills while cutting income taxes. At the same time enormous IOUs were undertaken by private Americans and corporations buying other businesses.

Abuse of executive power reared its ugly head once more. In trying to carry out foreign policy as it saw fit, members of the Reagan team sought extreme methods of maneuvering. On one occasion an assassination booklet was published for the Nicaraguan rebels. Mining of their harbors was performed. In an arms-for-hostage deal gone sour, subterfuge was undertaken by everyone involved, from military to private consultants to middlemen.

AIDS enters the vocabulary of the planet. This

disease had been compared to the most destructive epidemic of the past, the Black Plague, in its initial stages. Confusion reigned supreme as this affliction struck heterosexuals in Africa (its area of origin), but mostly male homosexuals in America. There was some panic in those already fearful and ignorant of this lifestyle. It gave rise to increased discrimination side-by-side with hysteria. Drug abuse also was found to be connected to the AIDS virus, especially for those injecting it into the veins.

As women libbers pushed for their legal rights, they ran into brick walls. Abortion clinics around the United States were picketed with the fervor of sit-ins of the 1960s. This time the protesters were ordinary members of Christian religious sects. A small number of radicals took things into their own hands, bombing a few establishments in various locales. (They claimed to have been told to act by God.) The Equal Rights Amendment, an attempt to add "sex" to the civil rights laws, failed in the 1970s and remained in limbo. Men resisted changes in the workplace that would permit greater female intrusion into traditional domains. Even male private clubs were being forced to open their doors and memberships to the opposite gender. (Blacks and gays suffered impediments as well.)

The 1980s have witnessed an intensification of natural disasters. Massive earthquakes have caused much death and property damage in Mexico and the Soviet Union. Mount Saint Helens blew its head off (literally) after awakening from a deep sleep. Flooding and heavy rains crippled areas of the Pacific and eastern Asia. Earth tremors rattled vicinities of the continental United States that had been quiet for 100 years or longer. Unbelievable catastrophes resulted in trains and planes killing hundreds of thousands of people in every corner of the globe. Even a Space Shuttle exploded after blasting off from Cape Canaveral.

Scientists continue to delve into new fields of inventiveness and old standard endeavors to bring forth novel concepts and fresh applications. Superconductivity and fiber optic technology stand out as two innovations that will help recreate civilization. They represent speed (via levitation of people and things) plus light (as a vehicle for unlimited information) as transmission paths that will carry humanity further in its quest for destiny.

The 1990s will prove to be an era of burgeoning chaos. Biological systems will experience it. There are numerous other examples of this in every field imaginable. Planets and human societies will demonstrate similar activities. The state of chaos is reached when a system begins to approach a crossroad in its stage of growth. Bifurcations result, which basically represent various paths leading to the next phase. Most of them are dead ends. Only a few are viable in the long run. But the consequences of this process move everything forward, including the understanding of what it means to be human and its place in the cosmos.

Destruction of the Myths

From the beatniks to the hippies to communal living to women's changing roles to transvestites and gay lifestyles, the twentieth century has witnessed an explosion of change that has rocked the foundations of traditional cultures. These and other social bifurcations are making a statement about the point in human history that has been reached. New myths must now replace the old if the civilizations of men and women are to survive. But more than this, mature perspectives have to lead the way.

Americans have been raised to know their

enemies. Within society good and bad groups of individuals easily can be identified. Stereotypes and labels were fashioned to allow such recognition. They were spread in literature, through words, and via the visual arts. But they were being torn apart as the decade ran its course.

Think back to when "Communist" was a dirty, ungodly person. Hearings were held to weed them out of all avenues of America before they twisted everything that was good and Christian. Switch to 1987 when Ronald Reagan seemed to change overnight from calling the Soviet Union the "Evil Empire" to his embracing Mikhail Gorbachev in Red Square as a friend. What happened?

Human consciousness truly is growing. Stereotypes are simplistic ways to view the world. After speaking with his opposite number and getting to know the Russian leader, Mr. Reagan did not convert but opened his mind through personal interaction. He can be praised for this major step in his life, for it adds to the process that the citizenry currently is experiencing.

The idea that all blacks are lazy or inferior to whites has been propagated for centuries. George Washington Carver, founder of Tuskegee University, must be an exception. How about Barbara Jordan, the former congresswoman from Texas? Then there's Jesse Jackson.... The black community is prospering. They're overcoming obstacles. (It's not commonly known that twice as many whites as blacks live in poverty.) Another myth is falling by the wayside.

Presidents, being human, get caught up in the same traps as do their governed. Libyan Moammar Kaddafi is one of the bad guys. When America feels the wrath of terrorism, the military strikes out if it can. Since the solutions for stopping such acts are complicated, an emotionally satisfying violent action

temporarily tempers the frustration of the population. Great powers take swipes at insignificant flies
on the wall of the planetary stage for such immature reasons.

Interestingly enough, Ronald Reagan rode onto
the American scene from the Wild West (California)
to make the world safe for democracy again. (He
and his wife do saddle up occasionally.) He led the
march to build up the military sector of government to strengthen the country. Weapons of war
represent muscle or power to dissuade by fear of
retaliation, which exhibits immaturity. "Might
makes right" as they used to say. The U.S. is right.
Therefore Grenada was a rescue, but Afghanistan
was an invasion. It all depends on your point of
view.

Terrorists, on the other hand, feeling frus-
trated, act out their hatred or hopelessness through
jihad, or holy war. They invoke the myth of a battle
of holy warriors blessed by their god to seek
revenge for wrongs that may be recent or centuries
old. Assured that a spot awaits them in heaven if
they die as martyrs, they readily accept what fate
delivers. This has been successfully applied in
Iran's war with Iraq. In addition, the U.S. as the
"Great Satan" was utilized in the earlier revolution
that ousted the Shah.

Since time began authority figures effectively
have used myths as the basis for protecting the
nation or going on the offensive. Today capitalism
and communism depict the two great myths of the
modern world. Citizens of these systems have been
taught to defend their governments at any cost,
including the total destruction of both sides. "Better
dead than Red" is a common expression in the
United States. The Russians are sure to have their
catch phrases as well.

Of course if such a catastrophic encounter

should start, what about the other life forms inhabiting the Earth sphere? Humanity's ego, placing so much importance on itself, could care less. As one peruses the technological civilization, many side effects (pollution, habitat demolition, and so on) have eliminated large numbers of the planet's lesser-developed forms of life--all of this in the name of some mythical progress promising a better way of life.

Americans scoff at Koreans eating cats or Hindus preserving the cow as a sacred animal. Is it imaginable to witness any member of a consumer culture participating in the potlash of certain northwestern American Indian tribes? (The total accumulation of their wealth is burned.) It sounds like something business would love, but is it affordable?

Myths do have a place in a society. They tell a story that paints a picture of why and how the world and the cosmos operate. They are a set of explanations that sanctify the social order and give its members a map of life's path. Security and identity are established.

Every element of the culture can be used for positive or negative purposes. From technology to science to political or religious philosophy, such stories provide ideals transformed into earthly connections. Atomic energy lights homes and also has the power to destroy. Spiritual teachings have been the basis for the Amish as well as the People's Temple. The practical application is dependent upon how it is interpreted and implemented on a daily routine.

Selective blindness and rigidity are the pitfalls of any mythology. By encouraging people to follow the faith of those who originated the teachings or writings, individuals find it too ambitious a task. After a while the mythology becomes inflexible and cannot deal with fresh perspectives or circumstances. When radical change is required to cope with a natural disaster, military defeat, or technological innovation, the mind and the system fail to adapt.

History teaches these lessons. The Aztec and Incan civilizations were conquered due to their mythology. Cortes and Pizarro came according to ancient beliefs, as the white gods who had promised to return to their people. In welcoming these visitors with open arms the indians sealed their fate. Conquest replaced celebration. The temples were looted for their precious gems or metals while the people suffered massacre.

Volcanic island inhabitants have worshipped their mountain spirits for centuries. Any rumblings indicated the displeasure of the gods. Primitive cultures also have considered storms, flooding, earthquakes, and so forth as an expression of anger of those spirits. Many peoples perished rather than relocate to safer locales when the Earth unleashed enormous energies.

Other civilizations went the way of previous examples. Nations throughout history in Europe and Asia, whether for crusade or colonization, radically were altered or reshaped with new myths via military vanquish. Christianity usurped Buddhism and Animism. Islam supplanted Christianity. Ownership of land collided with stewardship. Wealth as social status took importance over the personal character of the individual.

Now technology threatens Western mythology and the very fabric of civilization. Atomic, biological, or chemical weapons are the most critical of inventions with which leaders have had to come to grips. The average person on the street is being assailed by the improvements in every walk of life.

Medicine illustrates this to perfection. Americans believe that doctors literally are gods. This field is so complicated that an ordinary person cannot understand the intricacies of the body and its treatments. Whatever is said to the patient is taken as gospel. As afflictions amplify, so, too, have malpractice rates.

Insurance increases resulted from a myth that has been handed down to each generation. The medical professionals were thought to be able to cure all diseases and repair any injuries. Since in reality they are mere human beings, mistakes have happened. The physiology of each individual is unique. No one procedure or drug will affect every person exactly the same way. This also applies to elective surgeries, including cosmetic treatments.

Deeper questions relating to sexual interaction and the family are impacted by innovation. The taboo against sex between unmarried partners still raises the ire of those caught up in this myth. The idea of pleasure-seeking via recreational intercourse bothers these same people. Teachings always have revolved around a single purpose: propagation of the species as the sole reason for copulation.

Death and the definition of life came full circle when abortion and euthanasia became hot topics for discussion. Only the supreme being has the right to decide such issues, so the story is told. If humans start controlling these matters, there is a fear that the wrong standards would be implemented to limit or rid society of unwanted individuals or groups. Once the door is opened, of course, abuse is possible. The Hippocratic oath of doctors further confuses these issues, dictating a single-minded direction toward preserving life.

To resolve the abortion argument, societies have permitted women to choose, within varying frameworks. The staunch advocates of the mythical ideals refuse to rethink their stands. (To them it is blasphemous to even suggest....) With the march of technology, clinics may be replaced by a pill currently in production.

As far as euthanasia is concerned, machines now keep many people alive who would have died years ago. Nature no longer can take its course. Either the technology will lead to a bankrupting of the medical industry and force a change in its application, or individuals will alter their definition of death on their own.

At the other end of the spectrum, modern industries have spewed poisons into the environment. It is part of the "good" life. As the air, water, and food become increasingly tainted, more people are being born with genetic imperfections. Another consequence has been women with reproductive dysfunctions. Technology has attempted to correct these inequities.

Test tube babies have come to the rescue of some couples. Rather than taking part in the sacred sexual act to conceive children, male sperm and female ovum are combined outside the body. Although controversial, surrogate motherhood sets off a stronger alarm in the minds of the worshippers of the myth. It runs the risk of substituting love among potential parents to one of women as baby factories. For the physically impaired this has been a welcome added option. The whole mythical belief that partners are not fulfilled unless they have children has generated these debates.

Family structure has undergone its share of discord. In this age of disorder, instabilities have wrecked a high number of marriages. Communal living, mate-swapping, open relationships, and extramarital affairs produced bifurcations that upset the norms. The women's movement questioned the foundation of husband and wife roles. Man as the sole breadwinner and woman as caretaker have experienced a re-examination.

Family planning as a method for governing one's circumstances has been attacked as a vehicle to limit population sizes of minority races or religious groups. The myth of "go forth and populate the Earth" as a duty expected of the human family will not wane easily. When faced with famine or starvation, reproduction persists. And if the female is perceived as having one purpose--to bear offspring--no alternatives can be accepted within that mind-set.

Education is thought to be the major approach for creating any kind of cultural shift. But ideas alone will not change concepts that have been reinforced for generation after generation. It must be recognized as a way to communicate information. Time well spent in a classroom is overridden by the living environment to which the student returns and interacts within during a much-longer period of each day and year.

America's Great Society programs of the 1960s threw money at various social inequities. Low-income housing became ghettos practically overnight after construction. Welfare payments were mismanaged by those ignorant of appropriate priorities and proper budgeting know-how. Slovenliness turned sparkling, rebuilt neighborhoods into filthy covens. Given a home which they had no pride in helping to erect meant that other homes would be available when these fell apart. Vandalism contributed to the degradation as well.

Two myths are expelled in learning from these actions. First, money is a vehicle for improving conditions once a constructive plan is developed. It cannot be used in place of ascertaining the essentials of the problem. Those are always human in nature. Second, transforming the exterior of someone's environment does not alter the way he or she thinks and behaves. Material resources are only a means to an end.

Protests from the 1960s invoked the mythical concept that says if a group yells loud enough, if they cause a ruckus, things will change. This is very similar to a child throwing a temper tantrum to get what he or she wants. Just as many disciplinarians have accepted the myth of control through violence or fear, the expected took place. It continues today throughout the world in authoritarian regimes from South Africa to Chile.

One popular technique for eliminating unfamiliar neighbors, crime, and other burdens of life is interlaced with the myth of unlimited frontiers. Many Americans escaped communities in decline by moving elsewhere. With the changing face of immigrants and rapid development of the landscape, it is becoming harder to find safe places. Short or long-term travels (illegal in many instances) have taken on a worldwide movement of peoples to what appear to be economic and political havens.

Once again, these lands of opportunity promote increased productivity of material items as is necessary for progress to go forward. The result of this philosophy has been to excite those who accept this ideal and can be tricked into believing that anyone can be wealthy if he or she works hard. (Material prosperity is an illusion.)

People who acquire prominent positions fix the system so that it takes devious methods or crisis to change it. Therefore, the idea that a better mousetrap can be built is true. But if it threatens other manufacturers of that product, forget it. Two of many examples are the Tucker automobile and the 100-mile-per-gallon internal combustion engine.

Computerization and automation were said to be boons to the unfolding information age. With fallible human operators and programmers they have proven to be just the opposite. Less paper-work was to be generated. Instead there are hundreds of thousands of reams more. It would simplify everything from traffic light synchronization to billing procedures were additional promises made. The actual impact has been to complicate life to a greater degree.

Increased complexities have debilitated the feeling of personal control over one's existence. Some myths say that no one has dominance over anything that happens. They believe that God is watching every second of the entire planet's inhabitants' lives. Then there are the ideas that claim that all people are sinners. The Devil represents a third factor in this equation, playing on mental or physical weaknesses. (A recent Gallup poll revealed that 66 percent of Americans surveyed believe that the Devil does exist.)

All of this has had quite an effect in a particular nation. In a country based on individual rights, loss of command of one's life inflicts a terrible sense of hopelessness about the future and individual destiny. The overemphasis on the self has led to this state of affairs. The reverse is occurring in its adversary's nation, Russia, where the good of the whole is stressed as most important.

Human destiny is dependent upon reaching a balance between the individual and the group. Using a universal myth as a guide to restructure the communities making up Earth's unique diversity, the human family can find an infinite number of cooperative, growing arrangements that fit specific cultures present on this wondrous sphere.

Humanity, as a segment within the grand design, will learn to comprehend that the key to growth is through inner mastery. When its consciousness expands this one added step up the ladder of evolution, the New Age will have begun.

EXPRESSIONS OF THE ALL	EVOLUTION KINGDOMS	COLOR	MUSIC TONES*	NOTE DENOMINATION	SENSES	CHAKRAS	ENERGY
Matter	Mineral	Red	C	64th	Touch	Coccygeal	Atmospheric waves
Matter/ Energy	Plant	Orange	D	32nd	Taste	Sacral	Radio waves
Matter/ Consciousness	Animal	Yellow	E	16th	Smell	Solar Plexus	Microwaves (Radar)
Matter/ Energy/ Consciousness	Human	Green	F	8th	Sight	Heart	Visible light
Energy/ Consciousness	Etheric	Blue	G	One-quarter	Hearing	Throat	Ultrasonic waves
Energy	Astral	Indigo	A	One-half	Intuition	Spiritual (Third eye)	X-rays
Consciousness	Causal	Violet	B	Whole	Thought transference	Crown	Gamma rays

*Tones are in scale of A minor

THE ALL	COLORS	HUMAN EVOLUTION	BRAIN WAVELENGTHS
Energy	Red	Emotional	Beta
Matter	Green	Physical	Theta
Consciousness	Blue	Spiritual	Delta

TIMELINE

EVENT	TIME PERIOD
The All awakens, leading to creation of energy, matter, consciousness	The Beginning
Universes form	
Galaxies come into existence	
Earth's solar system takes shape	30 billion years?
Constant meteor bombardment abates on Earth (photosynthesis begins)	3.9 billion years
Kenora (first supercontinent)	2.3 billion years
Comet impact (oxygen holocaust)	2.2 billion years
Amazonia (second supercontinent)	1.5 billion years
Plants appear	1.3 billion years
Baikalia (third supercontinent)	800 million years
Ice Age (kills 70 percent of algae)	760 million years
Animals manifest	670 million years
Gondwanaland (fourth super-continent)	650 million years
Impact (destroyed 12 percent of all species; jawed fish and land life appear)	440 million years
Impact (kills 14 percent of all life; amphibians, reptiles, trees manifest)	370 million years

Impact (eliminates 96 percent of life; dinosaurs present)	250 million years
Pangaea/Lemuria (fifth super-continent)	220 million years
Impact (kills 12 percent of all life; mammals exist)	216 million years
Impact (marine and land life die; birds take flight)	138-150 million years
Global environmental revolution (modern mammals and flowers appear)	117 million years
Impact (primates result)	95 million years
Magnetic reversal	72 million years
Impact (11 percent of life and dinosaurs disappear; sea level falls for 60 million years; Atlantis develops)	67 million years
Magnetic reversal	24 million years
Impact (major mutations in ape and monkey species; temperature falls until 2 million years)	20 million years
Global volcanic activity at maximum	14 million years
Slow global warming initiated	2 million years
Impact and magnetic reversal (homo sapiens appear)	730,000 B.C.
Increased warming (Neanderthals present)	120,000 B.C.
Toba volcanic explosion (more powerful than Krakatoa)	71,000 B.C.

Climatic oscillations (human mental revolution)	71-56,000 B.C.
Impact (human communities)	25,000 B.C.
Extinction by overhunting	15,000 B.C.
Sea level has risen (Atlantis covered)	13-11,000 B.C.
First goat/sheep herds; accounting, record keeping well established)	9-8000 B.C.
Ur inundated (biblical flood?)	4500 B.C.
Dairymen present	4000 B.C.
Class distinctions evident	3600 B.C.
Jews exit Egypt	1050 B.C.
Religious surge and Greek science	600-550 B.C.
Birth of Christ	7 B.C.
Meteorite hits Mecca (Islam founded)	630 A.D.
Islamic science	1000
Krakatoa erupts	1883
Impact in Siberia/Russian revolution	1908/1917
A-bombs dropped on Japan/ United Nations established	1945
Ken Arnold sights flying saucer/ Jews head for Palestine	1947

DEVELOPMENT OF POST-ATLANTEAN CULTURES

Type/Location	Age for Introduction	Time Frame
Hunter-gatherers	Scorpio (Death/rebirth)	9300-3800 B.C.
West/Central Asia Borneo Australia East Europe Africa Siberia Americas		
Gardeners	Cancer (Nurturing)	7500-4000 B.C.
Southwest Asia Europe Indus Valley Nile Valley Antarctica Indochina Pacific Islands Americas		
Dairymen	Taurus (Bull)	4000-2400 B.C.
Mid East Africa		
Horsemen	Aries (Moving beyond limits of community)	2900-1250 B.C.
Asia Persia Antarctica Lower Volga River Eurasian steppes Southern Greece		
Charioteers	Aries (War, contest vehicles)	1250-250 B.C.
India China Aryans Western Asia Altai Mountains		

Blacksmiths   Aries   800 B.C.-1000 A.D.
                        (Forging war materials)
    Iran
    China
    Africa
    Etruscan
    Celtics
    Greece
    Phoenicia

Navigators   Pisces   1492-1859
                        (Water travel)
    Europe
    China

Astronauts   Pisces/Aquarius Cusp   1961-
                     (Visionary-led space travel)
    United States
    United Soviet Socialist Republic

EVOLUTION OF TECHNOLOGY

Era	Materials
Prehistoric 2 to 2.4 million years ago	Stone tools (crystal-- highest form of stone)
1.9 million years ago	Hand axes
120-160,000 years ago	High-quality tools
40,000 years ago	Sharp, delicate blades
29,000 years ago	Handles and spear tips
8-27,000 B.C.	Ceramics
6000 B.C.	Copper
4000 B.C.	Bronze
1200 B.C.	Iron
1888 A.D.	Aluminum

EVOLUTION OF GOD/ AUTHORITY
HIERARCHICAL FIGURES

Shaman

↓

Chief
Medicine man
Warlock/Witch
High priest/Priestess

↓

Oracle
Prophet
Priest-astronomer

↓

Emir
Sultan
Pharaoh
Caliph
Pasha

↓

King/Queen
Emperor/Empress
Czar/Czarina

↓

Pope
Imam
Bishop
Vicar
Rector
Parson
Prebendary
(Etcetera)

↓

Dictator
Premier
President
Governor
Chairman
Executive officer
Director

↓

(Future)
Counselor

↓

Self-directed

Chapter 2
The New Age

Esoteric philosophies teach that approximately every 2,000 years a new age dawns. At that time radical alterations become a part of everyday life. They include the injection of what were considered threatening concepts that present a renewed view of the workings of the universe. In addition, those beliefs expressed during the transition between ages are institutionalized as a new religion.

New Age Proofs

Historically there is a pattern to this change that began during the early Asian civilization and proceeded right up to the dawn of Christianity. This correlates with the astrological epochs that are designated by the signs of the zodiac. Science also lends credence to those not-so-unusual cycles.

Earth sciences have made astounding discoveries. The planet, as is commonly known, takes 365 1/4 days (one year) to make a complete journey around the sun. But how many people are aware that the North Star is not always in the same place in the sky? In fact, it has changed about every 23,000 years. In addition, the magnetic poles and the tilt on the axis have altered over 25,000-year intervals (the Chandler Wobble). There also has been speculation that the Earth's sun rotates around the star Alcion during this period.

Astrologers, on the other hand, say that each age occurs approximately every 2,100 years in connection with the zodiacal year. The time span involves how long it takes the Earth to travel through the influence of each of the 12 zodiacal signs represented by star groups in the heavens. To move through all signs corresponds to a 25,000-to-26,000-year cycle. Ancient Indian and Chaldean priests wrote about these computations, as did others. Between ages there exists a period of transition before the new innovations take place in society's mainstream. Old ways still continue on in those who fail to open themselves to the fresh knowledge and perspectives.

Over 2000 years ago, a variety of great teachers began preparing their cultures for a "New Age." The Far East and Middle East were the centers of world activities at that time. This led to the arrival of the one called Jesus at the break in the time line. Beginning in 600 B.C. an Era of Ancient Teachers was initiated.

Greece, Egypt, India, China, Persia, and other major global localities had reached a particular turning point in their civilizations by this period. The Greek states had commercialized their educational system. Egyptian god-kings disappeared. The restrictions of the caste system in India were strangling social advancement. Traditions of government and education in China had become stilted and inflexible. Persian culture and others faced the same basic problems. Some civilizations were in decline, others were stagnating or suffering external or internal disruptions.

Almost simultaneously, there arose numerous spiritual leaders and sects in these central areas at a critical time in the developmental process of the cultures. Since the basis for any civilization is a set of philosophical morals and values, they were due for renewal. In addition, the ideas surrounding how the cosmos operates and the human family's place in the "big picture" come from these teachings. They undergo cycles of innovation, literal interpretation, and refreshment as knowledge increases.

The *Kali Yuga* of early India, for example, describes such patterns. It mentions the requirement for avatars or enlightened individuals to make an appearance at specific historical periods. This enables the people to reintegrate their psychic lives with religious training. The *Bhagavad-Gita* of the Hindus speaks of a time when human virtue fails upon the Earth and the god Vishnu had to return. These same writings call 300 B.C. the Age of Avatars.

Spiritual teachers did indeed arrive in the nick of time. They possessed revelations about life or merely wished to assist their fellow men and women further in their spirituality. Every one of these leaders was a multidisciplinarian. They were competent in the fields of mathematics, astronomy, cosmogony, music, poetry, medicine, and philosophy. The only nonteacher was Lao tse, who held a high position in an exclusive library in China.

Both Lao tse and Confucius headed up the movements to reinvigorate Chinese society. Confucius fought for legislative and educational reform. Lao tse spoke to the disillusioned masses. Meanwhile, in India, Buddha pursued change in the caste system.

Pythagoras, during a transition of Greece into a union of states, opposed the commercialized approach to education that discouraged any discussions of morals and ethics. Zarathustra, the last of the Zoroastrian priests, preached the doctrine of the defeat of evil to the Persians. Christ, as the embodiment of God, demonstrated the complete mastery of physical life through pure spiritual development. (Symbolically, this represented the freedom from limitations.)

As a consequence of all of these extraordinary figures coming onto the scene, a long-term impact was made upon their cultures. Pythagoras paved the way for the great schools of philosophy, starting with the first formal academy (in his name) established in the Mediterranean vicinity. Buddhism produced an infusion of freshness into the universities of India. A Confucian school was founded in China that added similar vigor to that culture. In addition, great legal codes were devised in China, while astronomy advanced in both China and India.

Christ's teachings and the teachings of other avatars exhibit many commonalities. Speculation has led to the belief that several of these men exchanged information during their lives. It has been established as fact that Confucius and Lao tse did meet. There remain questions as to whether Pythagoras studied under Zarathustra or if he ever met with Buddha (although Pythagoras did visit India). Much of Christ's early years are a blank.

The lives of these great men portray the cycle of birth, death, and rebirth. Some died before any real visible change occurred. Others withdrew from society in frustration. Zarathustra was assassinated with a spear in the back. Pythagoras and

Christ became martyrs. Lao tse rode out into the Gobi Desert as a choice between the lesser of two evils. Confucius's heart was broken due to the lack of innovation in Chinese traditions. Buddha struggled with the reformation of Indian culture for 83 years. None of them lived to see how strong an impact their teachings would have upon each society. Two thousand years later their teachings still are alive, but faltering.

This is the point at which Planet Earth finds itself today. The "new world" beckons from the future. Most people fear what awaits them because it will rock the very foundations of their lives and disturb the beliefs and practices that have been drummed into their heads since childhood. This is truly a critical phase in history in which to be living, as it was 2000 years ago.

A New Age movement has sprung up in recent times in an attempt to alert those who no longer find meaning or application of previous religious teachings in their lives. This has happened because it now is appropriate for growth and development to move the human family to the next stage of evolution or progress. There must be a renewal of the old ways as a new comprehension of the cosmos and peoples' place in it enters every mind. The same process was incorporated into Christianity. As it unfolded it blended some of the past with fresh information.

Channeling

One phenomenon that has come onto the scene as a part of this movement is channeling. Individuals who possess this ability state that they act as a mechanism for nonphysical life to communicate with those ready to receive the enlightening concepts of wisdom. This is not by any means as unusual as it seems. People with this talent have been around since prehistoric times, and held the title of shaman. Some still are present in what are considered less-developed or uncivilized societies. Throughout history they also have been called priests, medicine men, oracles, messengers of the gods, mediums, or spiritualists.

Again, science is in its initial stages of explaining these abilities. Later on in the chapter, studies from the fields of psychology and neurophysiology will detail how it is performed. Suffice it to say that there have been thousands of individuals exhibiting this sensitivity. All human beings can do these things, but traditional science tells them that it is a nonexistent capability. Psychic abilities simply refer to an awakening of dormant faculties that will be a very real characteristic of the succeeding generations of the new age.

Paranormal Panorama

Other elements in this equation have proliferated throughout society. Near-death experiences, astral travel, clairvoyance, clairaudience, spiritual guides, and UFOs all paint a similar picture. The near-death experience has a common thread regarding traveling into a tunnel with a blinding light at its endpoint. Astral travel relates movements of the nonphysical self (soul) to any location on or off the planet. Clairvoyance and clairaudience pertain to the reception of knowledge previously unknown via nonphysical sources or entities. Spiritual guides, or guardian angels as some have called them, are nonphysical beings consisting only of light energy.

UFOs tend to express characteristics of all of these psychic phenomena. Reams of pages of material from nonworldly contacts have been transmitted by channels. Some abductees exhibited many of these fantastic talents immediately after their release or years down the road. Extraterrestrials claim to live in a nonphysical dimension, having to lower the rate of vibration of their bodies or spaceships to appear during their earthly visits. (Science also reveals that all atoms of physical matter do vibrate at specific frequencies measured in cycles per second.) UFO investigators have found evidence of visual sightings, ground impressions (for landing stands), and other indications that these craft are material vehicles that move within the atmosphere.

A portion of the channeled material states that there is a confederation of planets that functions in the cosmos. It is known that there are infinite numbers of stars with, very likely, planets revolving around many of them. (It would be egotistical to think that the Earth is the sole generator of life.) This leads to an additional concept of the New Age movement: individuals who can project their minds into the future. Psychic Edgar Cayce, as one example, was a channel who was able to go backward and forward in history as well as diagnose disease from a distance.

Star Trek Connection

One of many creative fields of endeavor involves writing. Insights are not limited to only a few human studies, as Einstein, Christ, and Jefferson can attest. Following from the UFO and space travel realms, Gene Roddenberry, creator of "Star Trek," is among such visionaries. He and his associates have portrayed the new age in its essential reality, in what it contains and how it orders the key events that must occur as the world to come will appear and operate.

The Age of Aquarius possesses two important

attributes. First, since it is an air sign, the influence of intelligence will predominate over emotion. That is indeed a necessary step to take in beginning to solve any problem. It also is needed to enable people to interact without letting words or stereotypes interfere with achievement of collective goals. Inventions and other advancements will come out of teamwork rather than individual breakthroughs in this era.

A second characteristic relates to the theme of the brotherhood of man. There is one human family on Planet Earth, and that is indisputable. Skin color and culture may differ, but all the physical functions remain the same and organs are interchangeable. Everyone wants the identical basics out of life: to live in human dignity, have control over their own circumstances, and have the ability to pursue goals through their particular means. When this philosophy is recognized and put into practice in the next age, a kind of millennium will have been born.

These and related traits are exhibited in the two television series (the original "Star Trek" and "Star Trek: The Next Generation") as well as the *Star Trek* movies. A global civilization of increased technology has blossomed on Earth, and the space program shows interracial crews exploring the unknown in groups (rather than the single or partnership pioneers of past centuries). Extraterrestrial contacts have permitted new worlds to be colonized under the framework of a federation of interplanetary magnitude.

Unification of the planet came about as a result of a not-so-unlikely occurrence. A group of genetically engineered superhumans attempted to conquer and bring together all peoples and countries. This is certainly a definite possibility with the advances being made in biotechnology. With the diversity and division present today, an event that forces the nations of the globe to cooperate for survival is perfectly rational. This is only one driving force that could bring the world together.

In one of the original episodes, there is a reference to the declaration of the brotherhood of man that spreads through the galaxy. It is exemplified by the crew and repeatedly affirmed during other shows. Any discussion of the subject centers on the fact that all people accept one another for what they are. The time frame of this exclamation of universal brotherhood falls within the approximation made by many astrologers.

Conquering space is an additional attribute of the next era (remember, Aquarius is an air sign). Besides spacecraft technology, a device labeled a universal translator has been invented. This should be no surprise. A number of researchers (Rupert Sheldrake, Albert Abrams, David Bohm) have written that the science of radionics points to a common vibrational relationship between all life that can permit crossbands of communication. Some of these investigators were pursuing this very important research in the 1980s. Interestingly enough, a part of these studies have been triggered by the phenomenon of channeling.

"Star Trek," no doubt, is one of many correlating subjects that point to the new age, and if the preceding was not sufficient there is another dimension encompassing everything stated previously. The joining of religious philosophy, mind sciences, and technology all have produced a civilization in which science and religion have merged. A final expression of this was portrayed in the "Star Trek: The Next Generation" series. In explaining what society is like to twentieth-century people rejuvenated from cryogenic suspension, they are told that every person does what interests him or her. Material needs have been satisfied. The basics of life are guaranteed and self-development and growth are the goals of everyone.

Future Lives

Psychologist Dr. Helen Wambach studied past and future lives, unveiling a number of correlations. Her subjects told of strikingly detailed elements of various lifestyles during ancient times as well as those yet to come. Although life in 2100 A. D. and further ahead could not be verified through records and artifacts (which did confirm past life recollections), all involved did relay similar consistencies.

She scrutinized two groups of participants while delving into future progressions. One set of hypnotized subjects possessed psychic abilities and had track records of successful predictions. They all related information about the turn of the century that corresponded to that of ancient forecasts. The 25,000-year cycles of planetary change, stated by many cultures throughout history, will continue around 2000 A.D. Much devastation from earthquakes, volcanic activity, meteor impacts, and other events will persist. It will be a period of great change.

In addition to this study, Dr. Wambach progressed volunteers into the years 2100 and 2300. She found that in the ordinary subjects, a regularity of conditions were described. By now the Earth had become barren, without vegetation. People lived in glass-enclosed cities. The population is five percent of what it is today. A space colony is in orbit and self-sufficient in agriculture, having its own seed bank. Food on the surface is artificial and bland.

Currently ozone depletion is a reality. No tech-

nological fix is available to replenish it. Even with
the newly signed international agreement on the
production and use of the chemicals causing the
problem, it only can get worse. The greenhouse
effect is warming the globe. Deforestation and
pollution continue unabated. A United States
government-sponsored research project even has
suggested a shift in the Van Allen Belts around the
Earth at the turn of the century. This alone would
singe the planet's land masses and everything on
them that was unprotected. (The water-fire cycles
of destruction taught by metaphysicians matches
such happenstance.) These factors and others are
indicators of this likely scenario.

Two innovations have been incorporated into
the inhabitants of 2100. There is no mention of
war, disease, or famine. This says that some catastrophe has struck and, in surviving, those remaining get along without conflict and strife. Also, life is
seen as a journey. Each person chooses to die
when he or she determines it is the right thing to
do.

In the twenty-fourth century (2300) the population has doubled (to ten percent of what it is at
present). Interplanetary travel has been a normal
part of the lifestyle of the times. Similarly, war,
famine, and disease continue in abeyance. The
philosophy of life still is associated with the journey principle and death as a single phase of the
grand design, as revealed from analogous sources.
The correlation between material from discoveries
over the last 30 years in seemingly unrelated fields
of science cannot be disregarded. After all, the division into narrow specialties has prevented men
and women from discerning the larger perspective
of what is called life.

The New Age is dawning. As change is a permanent condition, the time for reflection now is lim-

ited. The globe has become a collective waste bin for trash and toxic matter. The emphasis on how the planet works has not been a high priority. Meanwhile, the Earth continues to pursue its own growth. Along with it, many of the inhabitants are ready, willing, and actively searching to find fresh ways to enter the Age of Aquarius.

Shaman-Priests

Phenomena of the mind has fascinated people since time immemorial. The shamans of ancient cultures were able to perform extraordinary tasks. The members of their tribes stood in awe of them. An examination of distant past and recent history reveals that these feats and others have been a permanent fixture in every culture.

Shamans of all epochs were the mind scientists of their day. They could reach beyond the physical world in time as well as contact those entities (deceased relatives and spirits) in the nonphysical realm for wisdom. Deciphering universal symbols allowed them to perceive true reality and approach every day with an unparalleled clarity. As healers and counselors they had no match in their intermediary function between his or her peers and the nether world.

In order to be able to communicate with the "other side" or travel through time, these individuals had a variety of techniques. Some would chant, sing, and dance. Sleep deprivation, fasting, and hyperventilation also were invoked. The smoking of herbs or ingestion of psychoactive drugs, which they knew how to prepare for the desired effects, were additional routine methods. All of these triggered a specific area of the brain and put the shaman into a trancelike state.

Historical references tell of special people in

each and every civilization possessing these same powers of the mind. In Egypt, both Amenhotep IV and Akhnaton, rulers of their day, were said to have such capabilities. China and Japan had their share of shamans, which in the latter case were attached to the imperial court. Indian and Greek cultures believed in the afterlife, and the Grecian mystery schools with their oracles were well known. Both Celtic and Arabian societies exhibited parallel visionaries.

Christian Era

When the Christian era arrived, there was a drastic change in prophecy among seers in the Middle East. This occurred primarily because a new age was beginning. A renewal of the previous belief systems was in order and the understanding of life had to go forward. The greatest of teachers at this time was the one called Jesus Christ, although the name is not important. This shaman-priest in the eyes of his followers was seen as both human and divine (or existing in the physical and nonphysical worlds simultaneously). A single source now was believed to be the repository of all knowledge.

From the Dark Ages up until the mid-nineteenth century, the prevalence of Christianity overrode all other religious philosophies in the European sphere. But there were eminent soothsayers such as Nostradamus, Merlin, plus the Comte de Saint Germaine whose stature in this arena attracted kings and ordinary people alike. They were clairvoyants, clairaudients, and magicians.

Spiritualist/Modern Era

During the spiritualist era of the 1800s, only the

label affixed to those able to utilize their minds in this fashion changed. The term "medium" or "spiritualist" became common. They could talk to deceased relatives or famous historical figures who were no longer alive. The start of the modern paranormal epoch arose with the appearance of Edgar Cayce at the turn of the century. He could diagnose ailments at tremendous distances while in a trance. Cayce proscribed simple treatments (most of which worked) and later was able to transcend time, describing events, including the destruction of Atlantis, as well as his own reincarnation in the future.

Since Edgar Cayce there has been an enormous number of channels and those who can perform miraculous deeds. Jane Roberts acted as a transmitter for the entity Seth. Helen Schucman received the material for "A Course in Miracles," which was comprised into book format. Lazaris speaks through Jach Pursel with ageless wisdom both personal and planetary in scope. Elizabeth Claire Prophet, who with her husband, Mark, while he was alive, formed a spiritual community (The Summit) in southern California. Such living areas began forming around the globe in the 1960s.

Mind Science Discoveries

Scientific investigation of all of these related phenomena had its start near the turn of the century. Vast resources have been spent on these studies by governments, especially the military sectors. University research continues today mostly in the fields of psychology and neurophysiology. The discoveries to date are revealing functions of the brain/mind that are expelling old concepts and beliefs about the ways in which that organ operates at various levels.

Mind scientists of the early 1900s expressed analogous views regarding consciousness. They considered the unconscious to be a separate aspect of the mind's function that acts in a larger frame of reference. Terms such as the "subliminal self," "subjective mind," and "collective unconscious" were used to define it.

Going back to the late seventeenth and eighteenth centuries, Emanuel Swedenborg had related a similar comprehension in his writings. As a multidisciplinary scientist and mathematician, he pioneered these studies. Through his practice of yoga and self-hypnosis, Swedenborg traveled the invisible realms of space and time, meeting several nonphysical beings, including Christ. His conclusion was that thought is simply the transmission of information in the form of light energy.

In 1974 Wilson Van Dusen published his results after working with psychotics. He had spent 15 years employed at Mendocino State Hospital in California as a clinical psychologist. During his tenure, the clients he treated said much that reminded him of the writings of Swedenborg. They talked of hallucinations that fit Swedenborg's experiences. Their manifestations took the form of nonphysical beings that spoke through the patients. They described themselves as frightened or disoriented "spirits," fearing death as a result of curative treatments.

Two years before Van Dusen's book hit the stores, J.H. Brennan published *Experimental Magic*. In it he explained his investigations of occult rituals. Essentially he stated that these practices allow the participant to contact other entities, god forms, and beings that exist in the temple of the mind. Again, this material parallels that already discussed.

ESP research of the 1960s and 1970s concentrated on grand or general theory. This refers to individuals who can "log in" or tap into some source containing the information possessed by everyone. (It is no coincidence that these terms sound like computer language, as we live in a technological world.) Descriptions like this recall those of Teilhard de Chardin's noosphere (evolutionary envelope surrounding the planet), Jung's collective unconscious, and the akashic records.

Psychokinetic theory concerns the ability of the individual to move a physical item by thinking about it. In this field matter and mind are considered different from each other in the same way that the mind and brain are separate. However, all minds are of the same nature whether they reside in a physical brain or have not yet entered the physical realm. That means that just as the brain and mind interact, mind and other matter also must be connected.

Krippner and Ullman conducted experiments in telepathy during the 1960s. They found that while in the dream state, conscious subjects could transmit images to a sleeping recipient. In addition, Gertrude Schmeidler demonstrated that individuals who are open to new ideas are more likely to have paranormal experiences rather than those who remain skeptics.

Grof's LSD research interestingly shows many manifestations similar to channeling. These involved alternative states of reality, trances, changes in facial gestures while in trance, an unusual voice coming from a subject's mouth, the ability to speak a foreign language that the person could not repeat out of trance, automatic writing, possession, and the astral form of a deceased person entering the individual's body.

With thousands of experiments performed all over the world and so many correlatable events documented, the perspective of life that has extended through 2,000 years is due for renovation. But there is more startling evidence that has been revealed by the scientific mavericks of the twentieth century.

The first anatomical findings covering the human body and brain were made in the mid 1800s. Dubois-Raymond unveiled nerve forces to be essentially electrical signals. Helmholtz measured the rate of travel of these impulses at over 100 feet per second as they move through the body. Hans Berger discovered the electromagnetic nature of brain waves via his invention of the electroencephalograph in 1924. Forty-five years later, in 1969, David Cohen showed that brain waves produce a magnetic field inches above the head, which metaphysicians recognize as the aura.

Beyond the human vista, most spheres in our solar system, like our Earth, have an electromagnetic field as one characteristic. Dubois-Raymond has proven that electricity runs throughout the shells of all men and women. These impulses or waves are lower in frequency and weaker than those artificially generated broadcasting waves used in television and radio. This is because metals (for equipment, towers, and so forth) permit electricity to flow through them more easily than the material of a human body. But air, on the other hand, does not readily allow electrical energy to pass among the molecules spread out within the atmosphere.

Soviet medicine has a device that eliminates the need for anesthesia. It alters the electromagnetic field around a patient, putting him or her to sleep. Dr. Richard Miller has worked on very secret projects in the United States, one of which studied this topic. He indicated that his research involved changing the electromagnetic field around human subjects, resulting in altered consciousness.

Light travels in waves or frequencies that are outside of the range of vision of most people. Cosmic, ultraviolet, and X-rays are just a few examples. These can penetrate nontransparent matter; the human skull certainly fits this description. Channeled messages, in fact, say that the wise and spiritual element in the universe is light. General knowledge in this arena of science has revealed that the smaller particles of atoms (neutrons, electrons, protons, and so on) have higher frequencies of vibration. To go further, the brain contains cell walls with antennalike structures that can receive electromagnetic radiation of various wavelengths. The waves then are transformed into sound. Indications are that extremely low frequency (light) waves interact with, allow access to, and activate higher frequencies.

Cosmic Ecology

Recent studies have linked vibratory rates to everything on the Earth. From rocks and minerals to plants to animals to human beings on up to the planet itself, a connection exists between all of these. Each form of matter possesses a specific electromagnetic field and a corresponding frequency of atomic vibration. They are but two factors that comprise these organic and inorganic structures. Even the planetary ionosphere has a natural electromagnetic resonance matching that at which channeling and meditation occur (8 hertz or cycles per second).

Technological experimentation utilizing the higher centers of the brain has been in progress for decades. Metaphysicians state that the brain and spinal cord act as a television or radio receiver. This area contains both pineal and pituitary glands as well as the hypothalamus. They are known for certain functional vehicles (melanin, regulators of day and night cycles, and so forth). Scientists such as Michael Persinger, director of the Neuroscience Lab at Laurentian University in Ontario, Canada, have conducted tests that applied small doses of electricity to temporal lobe regions of the brain. Induction of channeling-like effects have been produced.

From time to time there are documented cases describing fantastic exhibitions of human strength. Some hit the news media because of their outrageous nature. Among these are events involving women or children lifting a car off of a family member when it slips off the jack while being repaired. Sometimes there is no recollection by the person who performed the feat. Science recognizes that adrenalin, activated by human emotion, is rushed into the musculature during this crisis.

Jumping ahead in time, a future in which people have the ability to consciously turn on and off these centers and others has to be on the horizon. What will society have to face when mind science is in the hands of the many and no devices are required to do this? The Age of Capricorn, 2000 years hence, is an era in which the key theme is "I use." In the present, where atomic, chemical, and biological weapons hang over the globe like a Sword of Damocles, the horror of their use is prevalent. The next epoch will challenge each person's self-control and responsible application of the ultimate power: the energy of the mind.

ETs Phone and Visit Earth

Ken Arnold's sighting of the first "flying saucer" in 1947 set off what has become a phenomenon of immense proportions. It has reverberated around the world throughout every nation. People in every profession, young and old, have been exposed to some aspect of the realm of UFOs. Yet it is perhaps the most controversial element of the paranormal.

Following Arnold's witnessing of this saucer-shaped vehicle and its associated unusual maneuverability, along came George Adamski with an even stranger tale of extraterrestrial contact. He claimed to be in communication with an entity from Venus in 1952. This being described an etheric plane of existence via telepathy. The Pope, President Kennedy, and other leaders were given information from Adamski that he had received in this manner. Eighteen countries awarded him, as did the Pope with the Golden Medallion.

Also at that time George Van Tassel told a similar story. His contact was named Ashtar. This entity explained that people's overtly material pursuits, plus the development of nuclear weapons, would lead to disaster unless a new direction was chosen. Ashtar spoke of a "spiritual millennium" that he had come to usher in on the planet. His mechanism for transmitting information proceeded via a lowering of his vibrational level.

This concept of living on a different plane has been a common theme among the nonphysical beings who have provided wise, enlightened messages to the individuals with whom they have spoken to or through. They mention their advanced spirituality and technology in their civilizations. This is used to permit them to physically appear or just communicate.

There are a number of small publishing houses that sell what seems to be an unlimited amount of written material concerning extraterrestrials, their home planets, how they live, as well as Earth's future. Guardian Action is the outlet for manuscripts from Tuella, who warns of catastrophes and related omens strikingly analogous to the Christian Bible. L/L Research markets writings that coincide with the Seth information. Seth promotes a reinvigorated humanity that emphasizes the level of consciousness or vibratory frequency leading to wisdom.

A confederation of planets and metaphysical teachings also comes forth from extraterrestrial sources. The purpose of the interplanetary group is to search out those inhabitants of the Earth who are ready to implement innovations (both technical and spiritual) for the betterment of all peoples. J.W. of Jupiter espouses communication by way of the pineal gland of his channel, Gloria Lee. The pineal gland is said to be the highest energy center (chakra) of the human body.

Since the 1950s so much has been written from other worldly communicants that it fills hundreds of thousands of volumes. In particular there are extensive correlations among contents in any one phase of UFO research. Investigators now are wondering whether there is an interstellar ESP station or channel. The previous information would indicate that this is true.

Finally, there is the specific case of Billy Meier. This hotly disputed contactee, a one-armed Swiss farmer, has been in and out of the international spotlight since the 1970s. He says that he first talked with visitors from the Pleiades star system (known as the Seven Sisters to astronomers) in 1942 at age five. A variety of human-looking space travelers have been dropping in on him in a somewhat cyclical span of time since that initial meeting. All communication happens via telepathy. The extraordinary aspect to these incidences concerns the still and motion pictures he possesses of the crafts that were filmed in the nearby Swiss hillsides.

Analyses have, like everything else, been roundly criticized by some and supported by other experts in this field. (This just goes to show that science is not an exact method for answering all of the questions of life.) The impressive factor in this case regards the enlightened and sophisticated talks people have had with a person having five years of formal education.

Meier describes the Pleiadean visitors as more technologically developed. They can move rapidly through space. But with that higher material knowledge, they demonstrate a maturity that people on Earth have yet to attain. On a home that is close to the size of this planet, they have a considerably smaller population. Pollution and war are not present. Each family reproduces fewer than three children, with three as the agreed-upon maximum.

What is astounding is the fact that they are led not by political officials but by a group of semi-physical (etheric) beings. These entities "govern" via advice and suggestion, as they truly are wise in thought and action. Metaphysical teachings convey that the etheric state is the next one after human existence.

UFO Significance

The phenomenon of UFOs and extraterrestrial contacts portends concrete changes for the residents of Planet Earth. It, along with all paranormal events that have permeated the media since the 1960s, generates key questions for every single man and woman wherever they live. As the New Age unfolds, those who have dealt successively with the personal and planetary inquiries (essential at this point in history) will take a step forward in their self-growth. Those refusing to change with the times will be left behind, as is obvious when one observes the cultural diversity existing all over the world.

Issues on the front burner deal with the very beliefs and traditional practices of each and every person. Is there more to existence than simply birth and death? What or who is God? Are there life forms who possess greater knowledge and technology than any civilization on Earth? Will human beings be the end of the line as far as evolution is concerned? Does life have a purpose? Can the brain perform miracles, including mind-to-mind communication, movement of objects without physical touching, and related magical occurrences?

There are further queries. Can individuals project their minds into the past or future? Have extraterrestrials visited the Earth at various times in history and prehistory? Are they walking among the rest of humanity today? Do extraterrestrial influences such as stars and planets affect human, animal, and plant life? What does it mean to be human?

Only at the transition into a new age (or in maturing as a species) would these questions be of primary importance to so many people at one point in time. For in uncovering the answers, a journey of unprecedented dimensions will transport the seekers into a world few can begin to imagine.

MIND SCIENCE DISCOVERIES

Experiment/Theory/Discovery	Finding
1. Temporal lobe stimulation with electric current	Out-of-body experience with profound cosmic or religious signifigance
2. Isolation tank (no external stimuli) (Lilly)	Subjects produce internally generated images and words
3. Psychically projected thoughts (images) to second individual	Correlated EEG brain wave responses
4. Antennaelike structures sticking up out of walls of brain cells (Barr)	Possible receptors of extremely low frequency radiation that are converted to sound waves by melanin
5. Schumann resonance of Earth's ionosphere at 7.8 hertz (Puharich/Persinger)	Facilitates human receptive systems
6. Brain generates impulses according to neurotransmitters regulated to neuromelanin (Puharich)	7.2-12 hertz frequencies are those measured during channeling
7. Activation of parasympathetic aspect of autonomous nervous system (Puharich)	Reception of telepathic signals
8. DNA comprised of preons (Puharich)	Permit interaction with extremely small-wavelength electromagnetic information across other dimensions of reality
9. Conscious escalation of energy exchanges between incoming energies to pineal/pituitary glands and pelvic gonadal region (root chakra) (Schwartz)	Increases brain cell activity allowing human senses to reach paranormal range
10. Synchronization of brain waves	Increased alpha range

Experiment/Theory/Discovery	Finding
in both hemispheres (Brown)	of brain waves (0.3-5 hertz); identical to twin telepathy
11. Shift in conscious attention (Millay)	Entire frequency pattern of brain waves shift to other frequencies similar to channeling
12. Flashes of insight (Scully)	Increased synchronization of brain hemispheres
13. Brain tuner (Beck)	Induces vibrational change in brain waves
14. Cross-band transducer (Meek)	Permits communication with the dead

---

RELIGIO-PHILOSOPHICAL EXPLOSION

TITLE	SPIRITUAL TEACHER	DATE
Taoism	Lao tse	550 B.C.
Zoroastrianism	Zoroaster (Zarathustra)	540 B.C.
Judaism	Deutero-Isaiah	"
Jainism	Mahariua	"
Numerology	Pythagoras	530 B.C.
Buddhism	Buddha	500 B.C.
Confuscianism	Confucius	"
Christianity	Christ	30 A.D.
Islam	Mohammad	622
Protestantism	Luther	1521
New Age movement (No single individual)		1975

STAR TREK/NEW AGE CORRELATIONS

	Age of Aquarius	Star Trek
Cause of end of 20th century civilization	Catastrophes driving people to mature and cooperate	World unification attempt resulting in much destruction that united Earth
Time frame	2150-4300 A.D. (Approximately)	23rd, 24th centuries
Themes and characteristics	Air sign	Intelligence over emotions; space travel becomes routine
	Group sign	Crew represents hundreds of people; United Federation of Planets
	Universal brotherhood	"All men brothers" is accepted philosophy
	Pursuit of self-development	Needs-based economics allowing pursuit of personal interests
	Science and technology	
	New ideas push back boundaries; fast-flowing energies	Space crafts that move at warp speeds
	Information and communication	Voice-activated computers
	Pictures	Records of ship's actions and explorations
	Psychic abilities become manifest	Universal translator based on vibratory frequencies; intuition as acceptable basis for decision making; transducer as key to technology

CYCLICAL AGES

Age	Date	Key Influences	Consequence
Scorpio	16,000 B.C.	Death/rebirth	Atlantean destruction and scattering
Libra	14,000 B.C.	Emotional instability	Palestinian culture begins
Virgo	12,000 B.C.	Hard work, organization	Rebuilding
Leo	10,000 B.C.	Kingly dominance	Kingdoms initiated
Cancer	8000 B.C.	Nature, inspiration	Growth of cities, record keeping
Gemini	6000 B.C.	Equality	Writing, legal systems
Taurus	4000 B.C.	Materialism	Creature comforts, luxury
Aries	2000 B.C.	Testing limits, breaking rules	Reinvigoration of all cultures
Pisces	0 A.D.	Messianicism	Infusion of Christian values, morals
Aquarius	2000 A.D.	Ego merges with cosmos, universal brotherhood	Reshaping of civilization into one human family
Capricorn	4000 A.D.	Break from past, total rationality	Science reigns supreme; loss of humaneness
Sagittarius	6000 A.D.	Harmony, balance	Cosmic integration
Scorpio	8000 A.D.	Death/rebirth	Inner self awakens
Libra	10,000 A.D.	Hard work, organization	Infinity as a challenge

Chapter 3
Mastery

Down deep inside, everyone has a lingering desire to understand what human existence is and whether there is a purpose to it all. Once one determines that that is the highest priority in life and unceasingly pursues those ultimate questions, the revelations follow. For each person that comprehension will be unique, and there may be difficulty in passing it on to someone else. This book was developed in just this manner.

Multidisciplinary Paradigm

A universal perspective can be obtained when a multidisciplinary approach is taken. Throughout history there have been great teachers and spiritual leaders who understood this. But beyond learning the correlations among philosophies and religions, a person must open his or her mind and total being to The All. When this happens, it is possible to connect at some level with the non-material cosmos.

The physical world and its associated sensual pleasures are fleeting moments of temporary bliss. Acquiring material items fulfills wants that are glamorized by society. Both of these produce partial satisfaction, but leave something missing inside the individual. A realization must be made that concerns this emptiness. Only through the maturing of the inner qualities (self-esteem, self-direction, self-confidence, self-love, etc.) can true gratification and completion be accomplished.

Arrival of the Masters

Religions that have been practiced throughout history began when a spiritual leader came into a specific culture. The purpose of the teachings was to enhance the lives of all members. Information brought forth was put into story format as a way of transmitting very complicated ideas to the majority who had not spent the time and effort developing themselves. This was a common practice appropriate for uneducated masses.

These extraordinary masters achieved their enlightenment through a life of celibacy. Abstinence was proof that they had gained control over one aspect of physical life. Other indications included long fasts to eliminate hunger, a solitary or collective lifestyle with like-minded people to concentrate on mastery (not to propagate dogma), and similar undertakings. The sole purpose of these practices was to tune into the cosmic (invisible) realm via a balancing of spirit, mind, and body.

After the great teacher moved on to the next level of existence, followers established a formal organization to dispense the material. Since it was considered the "Word of God," it had to be spread so that all people could know it. It was placed on papyrus in order to send it out and preserve it.

Rituals were devised along with the written word that permitted any interested person to achieve the greatness exhibited by the spiritual leader. As time passed, those rituals were corrupted as new heads of the sects lost the connotation of the symbology attached to the rituals. The information was perverted, similarly, after numerous mistranslations and deletions of certain specifics (due to current popular thinking). Literal interpretations of the material became the only way to read it when the symbols had lost their original meanings.

Every 2000 years unfamiliar enlightened men and women appear on the scene in the centers of civilization. They reinvigorate and update those teachings. Fresh insights help to propel the people into the future with a more advanced understanding of humanity and the cosmos. By then earthly inhabitants are ready and impatient to participate in the world in new ways. It is with these spiritual leaders that a one world order or era ends and the next is inaugurated.

These arrivals coincide with a decline in civilization. People and their leaders suffer through personal and social disintegration, having forgotten how their stilted religious dogma pertains to themselves and life as a whole. Global disruptions are a part of these events as well. At a critical point masters enter the mainstream to set things back in forward progression.

The Christ was a new age teacher. He did not come to put an end to all faults and frailties that are a necessary aspect of being human. What Jesus did provide was an example of a complete man who demonstrated via actions the path to personal transformation. It is only through this process that all larger social problems can be solved. Ethics and value clarification are at the center of behavioral and attitudinal change.

But the one called Christ takes on an even deeper representation, just as everything that exists can be viewed with various meanings. Stories can be seen as events with specific characters and circumstances. They may portray personal and social morals. Or there can be universal symbols that stand for ideas beyond human cultures. This latter reference is how the teachings and actions of this remarkable individual should be construed.

The key objective to life is to grow and mature. There is a next step up the ladder of cosmic progress from each level (mineral, plant, animal, human, and so forth). This is in keeping with the philosophies of all religions. The Wheel of Life described in Buddhism says just that. In simple terms it refers to the birth/death routine as a continuous process that occurs over and over again. At a particular point in one's development, perfection of sorts allows the individual to stop the material aspect of growth and concentrate on the spiritual or nonphysical. Christ accomplished this.

Metaphysical Analogy
(Or the Bible Made Clear)

Beyond the story detailed in Judeo-Christian manuscripts, there is a profound interpretation that can be understood through the analogies contained in those writings. Mary and the virgin birth is one example. Mary was raised in purity because she was chosen to be educated in the temple or church of her day. This was common among her sect of practitioners.

In esoteric terminology mother (of God in this tale) is a representation of matter. By giving birth she permits the father (God) or Spirit to take human (material) form in the child Jesus. Another view of this is the coming together of matter and

energy (or Spirit). It results in the birth of consciousness in the human form. Mary, in fact,
stands for this universal mother figure that in
other cultures produced Krishna, Buddha, Horus,
Ra, Lao tse, Zoroaster, Hermes, Plato, Pythagoras,
Zarathustra, and other god-men.

The concept of heaven is a universal ideal.
Mecca, Nirvana, the Jewish "homeland," and similar references throughout religion all describe a
state of mind. Christ himself said that the kingdom
of heaven was a place inside each person. This fifth
kingdom, in metaphysical teachings, is that state
of being that comes after the human world.

Even the birthing scene makes related connections. It is said that Christ was born in a manger.
This is highly suspect, because the symbol of the
lowest physical realm is a cave (for minerals). In
addition, the Essenes, who were the educators of
Mary and Joseph's employers (he was a priest and
probably named Zechariah), commonly were known
to have stone-covered rest stops for weary travelers. The bed of grass stands for the plant realm,
while the ass or donkey is the animal representation. As a child, the human or fourth kingdom is
established.

Astrology also figures prominently in this picture. The date of Christ's birth was celebrated at
137 different times of the year in numerous locations until 337 A.D. A decree by the Pope affixed it
firmly to December 25. On that date star charts
recognize that Sirius (the brightest star) was on the
meridian, Orion (the three kings) was nearby, and
Virgo (the virgin) had been rising in the east. The
winter solstice, occurring midway between the
autumnal and vernal (spring) equinoxes, deline-
ates the spot at which the darkest season has
passed and the length of daylight begins to expand.

There also is a relationship among stars and the

metaphysical Mary. Cassiopeia is recognized as "woman enthroned" or matter as the dominant force in the world. Coma Berenices stands for "labor of birth." Here matter is in conflict with spirit. Then there is Andromeda, in which the child rules (woman enchained) or matter takes second place to spirit. In the messiah context, Coma Berenices can be seen as the start of life and the balance of man, animal, and God. Finally, there is Bootes, meaning "he who shall come" in the Jewish language. All of these star systems are prevalent within the writings of these events.

Jesus (or "Johanan" in its original tongue) realized at some point in time that he was a true master. This refers to mastery over the triune nature of the physical world. The three wise men who brought gifts to the child display these same elements of the mental, emotional, and physical man. Gold has always been associated with the physical. Myrrh, being a bitters, has a mental connotation. Frankincense is the aspirational or emotional aspect. When these three have been mastered, or the individual possesses control over them, the spiritual quality awaits pursuit.

Christ's journey demonstrates this process. His baptism shows his conquest of those storms or tides of emotion to a high degree. Next, there were the desert tribulations he suffered. During a more than month-long fast he became extremely hungry, but refused to create food out of the rocks around him. He was tempted to prove his immortality by throwing himself off a mountain. Then he felt the urge to resolve all problems and eliminate pain from the physical world, which would have stopped evolution. These are the real lessons to be learned.

A third event pertained to the transfiguration on the mountain. Climbing a mountain simply refers to raising one's consciousness. It is attainment of mental purity or perfection. Who did Christ take to the top of this pinnacle? Peter, whose name means "rock," is a physical representation. James, who had aspirations of succeeding Jesus, is the emotional aspect. John knew God is good, or the mental nature of man who lived to spread the word.

Another trinity appeared to the three apostles in the form of Moses, Elijah, and Christ in all the glory of illuminated light. Moses, as the lawgiver, stands for the will of The All. Elijah, the prophet, actively was speaking the intelligence of The All. Love, as the third characteristic of The All, was provided on a daily basis through the example of Jesus. These six total expressions of The All are a blend of soul and personality resulting in a new state of being.

In order that this next stage be reached, a kind of death must take place. Otherwise, bondage by the physical realm has to result and a recycling back to human form will occur. Whether this actually happened via crucifixion or not really is unimportant. Recognizing that life is eternal, while changing states is the key mystery, Christ willingly left the physical plane. His final words prior to the transformation have been mistranslated widely due to a lack of comprehension of this allegory. The statement was "God, O God, How do I deserve such blessings?" Death occurred during the spring equinox, when a balance between light and darkness takes effect.

The one called Jesus now resides with the Spiritual Hierarchy. In this nonphysical domain of the cosmos live entities who oversee and assist lesser life forms without intervening directly, for they know that evolution is a long and arduous process that involves failures mixed with successes. Suffering and pleasures will persist at every human level. But as every master has said,

"These things and more will you do." This tells each individual that he or she can reach and perform even greater tricks or miracles when perfection has been achieved.

Going Home

As everyone masters this plane of existence, it will be appropriate to return home. Home is that non-physical part of the cosmos that has been given many names, all referring to the absolute state or perfection. The All has been used to designate this in the book. The Christ called it "death swallowed up in victory."

Planet Earth and its solar system will vanish into a never-ending recycling of matter and energy. New stars and their planets will take shape as the remnants of the past expand into nothingness. As the sun burns out and forms a black hole that collects cosmic debris for restructuring the universes in space, what was the next root race of man and woman will be a minuscule memory of The All. The Age of Capricorn has faded far into oblivion.

Capricorn: Beyond the Aquarian Age

Capricorn's era is linked to the idea of use. In the transition out of the Age of Aquarius, in which direct knowledge or connection to The All will predominate, lies dangers of unprecedented proportions. This will not be a world facing nuclear or other man-made catastrophes, but catastrophes of the mind. The sixth root race will develop what have been termed psychic abilities (sixth sense) by 4,000 A.D. Serious misuse of any information or capabilities can be minimized by coming to grips with the human issue of mature application.

At this time look for a new being to come onto

the scene. Mind power will entail influence over matter by thought. As the solar system travels further from the center of the galaxy, so too, will the atoms and molecules making up the human body grow increasingly sparse in their composition. The result is an etheric physique, one that is recogniz-able as human, but material objects can pass through like a hand in air. Metaphysical teachings back this up, stating that The All manifests itself in stages of evolution: mineral, plant, animal, hu-man, etheric, astral, and causal.

Astral and Causal Existence

The path of life outlined for humanity speaks of a semiphysical existence as the next step. These wise counselors will provide a hierarchy of govern-ment and rule by advice (reminiscent of the Pleia-dean society). Their sole concern will be to assist in beautifying the planet through an interconnection of activities by all other life forms. They will under-stand the complexity of the evolutionary journey and the universal laws of the cosmos. The human population will be united in its purpose to grow as well.

Following the etheric state the advancement continues to the astral stage. Scientific studies reveal that astral travel is reality and there seems to be a silver cord attached between astral and human bodies. This is amazingly similar to the string theory connecting universal matter that physicists have composed in recent years. This shows, again, how like concepts can be applied to seemingly unrelated items at various levels or planes.

Ultimately, the causal state is reached when the spiritual realm is mastered. The essence of hu-manity has grown into a fully realized being, or it could be said that total consciousness has arisen in a segment of The All. With these fresh experiences contained in The All, its development can proceed--for the few material things that the limited human vision can observe are but a scant amount of what truly surrounds everyone throughout the universe. Until people raise their standards of maturity, that which remains hidden does so to prevent the insanity it would wreak upon men and women. There is much to comprehend before humanity can look upon the vast expanse called the cosmos.

Chaos

Chaos provides a postscript to this discussion. Within life there are cycles of development in all species. Prior to the jump to that next stage, a crisis of disorder takes place. A number of mutations are produced that exemplify bifurcations or possible directions into which a species can evolve. Out of these come a minimal amount of new microorganisms, plants, animals, and so forth. The larger the symbiosis, the fewer mutations survive. In human terms this also relates to the various lifestyles that have appeared in recent decades. On a planetary scale it explains the erratic climatic and geologic events happening around the world.

Death is a type of chaos, whether used to talk about a solar system or a person. At this point in a physiologic sense, there is a breakdown in some subsystems of the body. They start to fail, succeeded by a disorganization and fragmentation in the cooperative functions they carry out in the human body. (Symbiosis is defined as a total integration of autonomous functions performed by numerous independent organs: blood, tissue, spinal cord, nervous system, brain, and so on.) The cohesion of the cells disperses. Even the primitive consciousness separates from each cell. Finally, thousands of individual testimonials of those who have traveled to the brink of death and returned relate experiencing joy and a bright light that immerses them when dying.

Perfection or Absoluteness

The solar system, too, has associated links that just now are being uncovered. Without the Sun and the planetary neighbors surrounding it in the exact arrangement that presently exists, life would be altered dramatically. Beyond this system lies Alcion, the star around which everything here revolves. And so on and so forth into the infinity comprising The All, for physical matter and non-physical energy in their never-ending expressions are parts and subsystems of The All.

Men and women are indeed created in this image. Humanity is an infinitesimal experience of these ultimate expressions. As people live out their lives, The All gains and grows. Energy, matter, and consciousness represent The All as well as each human individual. The All contains all of the information that will ever exist. It has accumulated it in part here on Earth, as each succeeding generation of life forms fulfills or fails to achieve maturity. Today it may seem that the human family never will reach perfection. When looked at in a 70- or 80-year life span, a very small perspective, it does seem impossible. But when considered in geologic time (billions of years), there has been much development all over the globe.

Yet it has been said that The All is perfect. To say that it is growing appears to be a contradiction. Using a human frame of reference distracts from such an approach. Time has been called the fourth dimension, and it is. The place where the United Nations building now stands was vastly different thousands of years ago--there was a far-different reality of life. The vicinity is in the same general longitude and latitude on the Earth. Visibly, only the landscape has changed. Other more subtle alterations have been made that may not be seen easily with the naked eye.

This planet has moved over those same thousands of years. It is now further from the galactic center than it had been, although the change is imperceptible on a cosmic scale. The All has given birth to Planet Earth and all of the uncountable star systems throughout the cosmos. Their deaths have occurred in the blink of an eye. This process has produced everything that can be known and experienced given an infinite amount of time (in human terms) to do it. The All's level of existence is one without time so that every event in all parts of the cosmos is happening simultaneously.

Comparing various life spans may also help comprehend this extraordinary view. Bacteria live only for minutes. An average person reaches age 70 to 80 before death occurs. Stars last billions of years. To most people this seems like infinity because it is well beyond human understanding. Angels or nonphysical beings have relayed through channels that, in all practicality, they live an unlimited length of time. They are the stage of evolution prior to the perfection of The All. The voyage of humanity must continue as space travel and its related technology provide new experiences and opportunities to expand the collective minds of everyone toward the goal of unity with The All. The mind sciences then will prepare all people for the final journey into the nothingness of the cosmos on the way to the home from which all life has come (completing the circle).

Chapter 4
Lifecycles

The secret to self-development, greater awareness, higher consciousness, or whatever label that is attached to this process occurs through multidisciplinary studies. Along with that must be a total openness to fresh or nontraditional ideas and information. This involves leaving every preconception about the intricacies of life out of this wondrous trip of discovery while listening to the inner truth that everyone possesses.

Separation of information into distinct subjects has an important place in any society at a specific point in its history. However, when finer and finer details become the prime pursuit of actors in their fields, it bogs down progress. Specialization and tunnel vision result. Mathematicians can no longer talk with physicists. Philosophers and religionists fail to find commonality of concepts due to dogmatic interpretations. The truth is that life is one big picture puzzle that becomes clouded by narrow perspectives.

Conflict and disagreement arise from the present methods of conducting all activities of structured societies. Unification of Planet Earth will occur when the ideal of cultural diversification is seen as paramount to the growth of humanity. Through unique ways of approaching life and ascertaining the similarities and correlations between perspectives, people will realize a balance of individuality and wholeness. From that point forward a symbiotic blend of the human family will develop into a planetary oneness, ready to take the next step up on the ladder of existence.

One such interdisciplinary example that can assist this advancement concerns lifecycles. They reveal themselves in everything men and women do. They are found on the sun, other planets, at the microscopic level, and on up the line. Their analysis and implementation in personal lifestyles and structuring societies will go a long way toward facilitating development of all life forms.

Previously, astrological and planetary cycles have been discussed. These reflected how grand historical changes are influenced by the Earth's motion plus extraterrestrial impacts. There are more interconnections than most people realize. Sunspots have appeared on the public agenda for a few decades. The Moon and its phases have likewise been examined. These are just a few of the events constantly taking place in the solar system.

Cycle Basics

Greek culture provides the origin of the word "cycle." It comes from "kuklos," meaning circle. In the context in which it is being used here, it refers to a sequence of events that happens continuously in the same manner. They recur in every aspect of personal, social, and planetary life. Some seem totally unrelated, such as the match of abundance of U.S. grasshoppers, the sales of General Motors cars, and the water level of Lake Huron. The key to their unraveling has been an interdisciplinary study of unprecedented magnitude.

Cycles have been discovered within almost every possible biological phenomenon. Activities of crabs, pigeons, and turtles, as well as cellular activities of rats and fish are cyclical. The growth rhythms of fir trees and mushrooms exhibit specific repetitive patterns. In addition, the unearthing of the same kinds of periodicity are becoming more clearly known in the physical sciences. Professor Giorgio Piccardi of the University of Florence proved, after considerable years of research, that extraterrestrial influences effect everything on this planet.

In 1958 Piccardi performed a series of chemical experiments that should have reacted in exactly the same way. But they didn't! He demonstrated that any reaction involving inorganic compounds was dependent upon solar activity, cosmic ray bombardment, and the season of the year. In a related test, Piccardi and a colleague determined that human blood coagulated more slowly under a copper screen (that blocked off external influences). This was confirmed in Japan.

Sunspots now fit neatly into the picture with regard to cycles in numerous fields of study. Disease epidemics occur twice as often at the maximum output of solar radiation. Cholera, influenza, diphtheria, and meningitis outbreaks all fall into these periodic patterns.

There are the familiar 24-hour days that correspond to the Earth's complete rotation on its axis. The Moon's day is approximately 25 hours (24.8). Research with insects and animals has led scientists to believe that even molecules behave in accordance with such cycles. Human blood pressure, temperature, respiration rate, mineral excretion, metabolic levels, urination, pulse count, flow of blood, and so forth are dominated by these forces as well.

Biorhythms were popular in the 1970s as a way to gauge intellectual, emotional, and physical highs or lows. The Chinese concept of *Ch'i* (vital energy flow) pertains to certain parts of the body in which that force circulates at a specific time. It is said to start in the lungs (at 0300), run to the large intestines (0500), and then on to the stomach (0700). The energy passes to the spleen, heart, small intestines, bladder, kidneys, pericardium (heart membrane), reproductive organs, gall bladder, and liver. Each area of the body has a flow of Ch'i for two hours before it moves on to the next.

Chronopharmacology has arisen in the medical field out of investigations of these physical cycles. It has remained a minor practice due to the huge increase in legal lawsuits against doctors in modern society. Try adding to current methods the idea of prescribing medicines according to body rhythms and fear sets in among most professionals. Yet it is well known that all drugs react differently depending upon time of day or night they are taken.

Animal studies link all life forms to earthly physiological rhythms. Atlantic oysters have been removed from the ocean and taken hundreds of miles inland, where they continue to follow circadian patterns. Hamsters, kept in isolated rooms with artificially controlled day/night cycles, produced data different from that related to the altered lighting conditions. Their activities sped up four days after a full Moon and one or two days before a new Moon.

Obviously some people are going to remark that all of this is mere coincidence. But when the abundance of Canadian lynx and muskrat populations, Arizona tree-ring widths, English financial crises, and the barometric pressure in Paris fluctuate together in cycles of 9.6 to 9.7 years (and in phase), coincidence has to be ruled out.

Human Lifecycles

To begin with there are individual cycles as a part of living on this planet. British researcher Joe Cooper, working in conjunction with Dr. Alan Smithers, investigated 35,000 birth dates. They found a statistical correlation among seasons of the year and the eventual professions of those individuals. Soldiers were born in midsummer to late autumn. Early summer to mid autumn was the time of birth given to doctors. Artists came into the world during late winter to late spring. Musicians arrived in late autumn to mid spring.

Morning and evening people do exist. This has been proven by studies relating that those most alert in daylight hours have their highest body temperatures at those times. Night people display the opposite trait. As a follow-up to this research, the participants switched sleep patterns without changes in temperatures. (Creativity cycles operate on a 7.6-day and seven-year routine. Check Steven Spielberg's *Star Wars* trilogy and others.)

Emotional ups and downs have a basis in fact. For men they run from elation to depression and back to elation again in five-week cycles. Women, due to their menstrual period every 28 days, demonstrate an amorous cycle recurring every 14 days. There is an increase in sexual desire just before menstruation and again eight to nine days after the cessation of the menstrual flow. Interestingly enough, this agrees with the Jewish concept of having 12 clear days after menstruation before the next union takes place between man and wife.

Electricity is a definite element of life. The

human body has this and other forces flowing through it. Four electrical cycles comprise each individual. These function daily, bimonthly, quarterly, and semi-annually. During these periods electricity is streaming through the anatomy. As all forms of life are related, tree voltage outputs regularly occur at six-month intervals.

Weather Cycles

Weather conditions are a constituent to this big picture. Studies in the health sector have shown that some kinds of depression and other afflictions are triggered by sudden changes in sunlight, humidity, barometric pressure, and temperature. In like fashion it contributes to the interactions of people on social and planetary scales. Records from tree rings and geologic sources (core samples of soil and ice) display routine alterations in climate and atmospheric status on the Earth.

Four 100-year weather cycles coincide with four basic models of social conditions. In cold/dry periods individualism, weak governments, migrations of peoples, and mob action prevail. The warm/wet eras exhibit the organization of achievements, an emphasis on cooperation, integration of views and efforts, plus government becoming more centralized and rigid in their operations. Warm/dry climes are associated with despotic governments, police states, individual behavior becoming increasingly introverted, as well as a decline and depression in economic systems. A cold/wet epoch features individualistic philosophy being written or espoused, decentralization of government, and anarchy during the period's climax.

American history, among other histories, falls neatly into these cycles. The Revolutionary War, the Civil War, and the civil rights movement all occurred on schedule within this framework. The panics of 1793 and 1893 correspond with this routine, as did the depressions of the 1830s and 1930s. Presently, observing these and additional past events, the future can be foreseen, as this country and the world progressively deal with the same issues continuously.

The 1980s was a decade when individual behavior patterns became introverted. AIDS, drug abuse, and their moral backlash invoked a call to "return" to earlier days of morality.

In some cases laws (discussed or passed) and government enforcement of those laws already on the books took on an almost police-state bent with regard to personal activities. A stock market crash occurred. Trade problems were at the top of the nation's agenda. Drought struck. All of this in a warm/dry climate, according to the scientific community.

Social Cycles

In the United States there are additional explicit cyclical events. Church membership and attendance increases every nine years. At the same time savings accounts reflect their lowest sums. In contrast, as savings increase church attendance falls within a similar time frame. Another factor that may cause church membership to burgeon is that deaths have been shown to go up accordingly (every 8.92 years). Obviously this explains the essential securities of men and women: religion and money.

Crime patterns are discernable when scrutinized. Murders increase during the hottest months (July and August) and at night and on weekends. The previous statistics relate to rape and aggravated assaults. Robbery is higher between 6 P.M.

Saturday and 2 A.M. Sunday in the months of December, January, and February. The month with the least crime is May, which is highlighted by a large number of dog bites.

Human unrest covering the period between 500 B.C. and 1922 has shown phases ranging from initial states of normalcy to revolution in 11.1 year cycles throughout the world (reminiscent of sun-spots). Every regular cycle has subcycles into which it can be divided. Beginning with three years of stability, peaceful tolerance is the rule of thumb, as citizens go about their own lives under the autocratic government of minorities. Next, there are two years of increased excitability as revolutionary leaders come onto the scene. Although three years of revolution and war follow, splinter groups unite behind one charismatic person. Anarchy is the prevalent result as the violence continues. Out of this chaos has come democratic and social reform, as well as solutions to the most pressing problems. Finally, a decrease in activity is witnessed over a three-year period, resorting back to a calm inertia characterized by apathy.

War also falls into regular intervals. Historical records reveal a 142-year cycle of international battles repeating with intensity. Initially, every 71 years there are a greater number of conflicts, succeeded by the same time frame of lesser amounts. The twentieth century has demonstrated this fact. Between 1914 and 1985 there has been a high degree of fighting among nations or surrogates supported by a third country. Currently a reprieve is in the works that will last until 2056.

Subcycles are a part of every pattern. Links to other arenas also can be determined. During a 9.6-year interval, an abundance of certain animal and fish populations can be counted. Two examples are the Canadian lynx and New Brunswick salmon.

Obviously there is a limited amount of food (or other raw materials), so a reduction has to accompany this overpopulation at some point. A warfare/ excess population connection can be seen as a throwback to ancient tribal life that remains deeply imbedded in the collective consciousness. New reasons are outwardly promoted as the cause for these violent actions (political philosophy, potential invasion, and so forth).

An economic subcycle also is related to that of war. In a 17.7-year period there is a topping out reached in production. It is at these regular peaks that conflict between nations hits an overall high. Consider United States activities in this field: Spanish American War (1898), World War I (1914-1918), World War II (1939-1945), Korean War (1950-1952), Vietnam War (1960-1973), and the Nicaragua conflict (1980s). Approximately every 18 years the U.S. industrial production crested at the height of war. (Figures used are statistical averages and do not match each and every pinnacle, but are very close to it.)

The complexity of life is such that there are all kinds of repetitions of history. They never are exactly the same, but parallels do stand out. Astrology's correlations with the historical record amazingly show recurring global activities in waves of 164 years. Each wave is influenced by a particular star group or zodiacal sign. Remember the old adage, "We are doomed to repeat history if we fail to learn from it"? In understanding these parallels, sufficient information can be known about what the future holds.

The 1990s

Bordering on the eve of another cycle, the 1990s will possess their share of unpleasantness. By

1993 a financial panic is due. Its worldwide effect will dwarf the previous four panics. An innovative credit system, ready to go into effect in the Common Market countries by then, may soften the probable banking devastation. (Debit cards have been used for a number of years on many parts of the globe and slowly are creeping into the credit card industry.)

This augurs an unsuccessful one-term presidency for George Bush. Although honest and hard-working, the dangers and dilemmas of this four years will be mostly out of his direct control. His administration will be beset by little fanfare and cooperation in dealing with the issues of the day.

Along with the banking and other economic problems (Third World, consumer, and federal debt), the crises that are building are going to be difficult to get consensus to resolve. Our declining environment cannot be replenished easily since the backbone of the industrial system is fossil-fueled. So, too, of course, is transportation, heating, and cooling machinery. The ozone layer will continue to erode and the greenhouse effect worsen. All of these conditions combined will add famine and hunger to the developed nations.

In order to cope with these immense challenges, it is important to realize that a constitutional crisis will arise as things continue to deteriorate. In 1992 a change of the party in power is assured. A perfect parallel to this is that which occurred back in 1828 when similar (but less drastic) circumstances were in effect. At that time Populist Andrew Jackson had defeated incumbent John Quincy Adams. Jackson formed a coalition of the disenfranchised citizens and those with falling standards of living. Who is presently solidifying his Rainbow Coalition and came close to winning the Democratic nomination?

As this country is divided increasingly between rich and poor, a true leader who can bring people together will be needed. Without stimulating leadership (Bush), a charismatic figure is required. Such a person will encourage the nation to meet the necessary challenges. A combination of preacher and statesman must establish himself by the 1992 election. The current political field seems to imply that Jesse Jackson is that man.

The severe pressures upon that new president will go far beyond that which took place in the 1930s. Just as FDR was faced with a fascist's attempt to overthrow his administration, so will the one elected in 1992. As problems strike one on top of the other, an authoritarian regime will be seen as the only way to get a hold on the crises. Certain widely accepted constitutional rights may be suspended. But there are additional dangers with which to come to grips.

With the conclusion of the final decade of the century, expect great natural disasters to befall the planet. This is the finish of another cycle, lasting over 12,000 years (when Atlantis was covered by a rising sea level). This is exactly half of one zodiacal year. The Chandler Wobble is due to reorient the Earth on its axis. Indications from various sources foretell of miraculous events as well as unprecedented catastrophes on an enormous scale. (Dr. Richard Miller also has participated in a secret U.S. government research project that resulted in the unlikely scenario of a shift in the Van Allen radiation belts surrounding the planet by 2020.)

Since 1970 a variety of unusual geologic and climatic events have taken place. A new tornado alley has appeared in the United States. Volcanic activity around the world has proven that these very explosive sleeping giants can indeed awaken from centuries of hibernation. It even has snowed in southern Florida. Torrential rains have inundated many areas of Planet Earth beyond the norms of recent eras. The earthquake in Armenian Russia, plus the one a few years earlier in Mexico City, are merely signs of what is to come during the transit from one age to another.

The year 1992 is significant for many reasons. It represents the five-hundredth anniversary of Columbus' journey to the New World. The European community will become a single economic unit. The first country to abolish slavery, Denmark, did so in 1792. The ruined city of Pompeii was discovered and the plague had wiped out 15,000 in London 400 years earlier. During the voyage of Columbus, Jews were being expelled from Spain for not converting to Christianity amid the Inquisition. In addition, the book publishing profession was established as an occupation.

These historical facts project numerous exciting experiences. A new space discovery will be made in 1992. It may well be the first unquestioned picture of a planet circling a star out in the far reaches of space. The Hubble telescope will be in orbit around the Earth by then, enabling scientists to see farther than ever before into the galaxies of the universe.

Watch for the total abolition of apartheid to come to pass in South Africa as the decade closes out, as many citizens are of Dutch ancestry. The lost continent of Atlantis will be, once and for all, revealed by scientific evidence.

AIDS, as a threat to the population at large, will have killed tens of thousands in one major city in the world (most probably New York or Los Angeles). The Middle East will surge in conflict as the Jewish-Palestinian issue heats up again. The publication industry has been suffering through an overwhelming amount of book submittals. The only solution is a massive increase in home or local corner desktop outlets.

All energies released, as is evident from the preceding, will not be destructive. Spiritual growth opportunities are going to be available in unprecedented levels so that each person ready to move forward can do so. Churches will reinterpret their origins and teachings. Psychic abilities, miracles, and healings are sure to proliferate. A reinvigorated view of life produces fresh ways to see the cosmos and our place in it.

The Twenty-First Century

Contrary to what some new agers believe, the beginning of the next century does not automatically usher in the Age of Aquarius. Continual arguments between astrologers has yet to establish the arrival of this epoch in human civilization. The present Age of Pisces will be completed when permanent underwater cities for work and living facilities are in place.

An Aquarian influence is to provide the perfect stimulus to assist the entry into the 2000s. Following on the heels of the last decade, things may seem bleak. The negative aspects of Aquarius indicate continued conflict from those not yet prepared to change their thinking. Power centers are controlled by individuals who will not give up their positions easily, if at all. Social reform is always a part of this zodiacal sign, indicating that it will proceed. In those states and nations not resolving to make needed changes prior to the turn of the century, violence and suffering are going to cause upheaval.

Other nonhelpful characteristics that may express themselves during this wave are an overdependence on the group, extreme sensitivity, indulgence in mystical fields of endeavor, and inertia. Add to these disloyalty, opportunism, as well as shortsightedness, and there could be much distress.

However, due to the information contained in the *Kali Yuga*, a positive Saturn influence will rule over the 1998 to 2003 period. Its impact dictates persistence, endurance, and prudence to prevail. In conjunction with these attributes, management skills in the military, government, business, and religious sectors are sure to reassess, then transform, operations. (The *Kali Yuga* of ancient India calls this the start of a thousand years of peace.)

From 2003 to 2010 Neptune's bad side will be the causative agent for exaggerations of good and evil at personal and planetary levels. Eruptions of turbulence are expected. People will tend to do things they are unprepared to control, and regret them at a later date. Drugs and alcohol, or similar consciousness-altering substances, may lead individuals seeking to expand their understanding of the cosmos to irresponsible deeds. Chemists and related professionals are the ones to keep an eye on in that future time. New dream merchants are going to be on the scene as well. In addition to the previously emphasized description of this period, expect fanaticism and delusions to drive the activities. Along that line, groups and solitary souls will use any means to gain irrational goals.

History demonstrates examples of past Aquarian waves that reflect what is to come. In the 1830s and 1840s there was a true age of reform. Everything from institutions in charge of mental health to women's rights to child labor to governmental operations all were upgraded. Literature of the day had the pursuit of perfection as a theme. Unionization began in Germany and spread. Since Aquarius also impacts the scientific community, advances in electricity, the telegraph, and an initial computer (analytic engine) were made. In addition, the Mayan civilization was unearthed for the first time.

In the same period, though, conflict did show its ugly head. Andrew Jackson, as U.S. president, collided with the banking industry, producing a depression. Napoleon Bonaparte attempted an escape from prison at Strasbourg, resulting in bloodshed and his expulsion to Ham. The U.S./ Mexican War occurred at this time. Riots in England arose in its industrial north. Even P.T. Barnum's first "freak" museum opened in the 1840s.

In the shift from Aquarian influences to that of Pisces during 2010 to 2011, similar events are sure to occur. From 2011 to 2017 the fishes are indeed tugging in opposite directions. Under the auspices of this, wholeness can be grasped as well. The grand design of the cosmos will continue to be unwrapped. This includes the intricacies that compose the big picture. If applied to education it translates into a more multidisciplinary approach. It is a time of visionaries and romantics above all else.

On the opposite side of the coin, this epoch may be one of childishness and irresponsibility. Discontent and feelings of victimization could spread among the populous. The result of that type of behavior on a large scale means a withdrawing of people or a retreating from reality. Disorganization may well be the ultimate state of global conditions. Likewise, a force messianic movement to redeem others could lead to a personal and planetary disillusionment as advancement.

Mercury's positive side indicates that the years 2011 to 2017 are likely to be ones featuring new beginnings. Conventions will be uprooted. Changing attitudes must rule the thinking of men and women. Inventions are going to be made at a steady pace. Computers and communications reign supreme as breakthroughs come into everyday life. The fields of teaching, secretarial work (automated and voice-activated typewriters), travel, journalism, education, carpentry, engineering, and medicine also stand out.

The next few years, 2017 to 2024, have a negative Venus dominance. This spells laziness, indecision, excessive romanticism, impractical attitudes, and carelessness as prevalent characteristics. With femininity, art, and beauty prominent in society, pleasure seeking through fulfillment of desires is bound to be on the average person's mind. Business and social issues will be intertwined.

This future period undoubtedly will be the final stages of the Piscean Age. As a water sign, as well as noting two forces pulling in opposite directions, Pisces meets the criteria for transiting into Aquarianism. By now undersea abodes and businesses are going to be in the construction phase, if not functioning. Foods from the ocean (from innovative sources) will fill dinner plates. Thermal energy from the water's depths is sure to be more fully developed. A religious revival will be emphasized, stirring fresh perspectives from old tired beliefs.

A perusal of the last Piscean wave of 1847 through 1861 reveals traits related to those described. Most European nations were torn apart by revolution followed by a rebirth in their societies. Marx wrote his *Communist Manifesto*. The slavery issue remained unresolved during three consecutive presidential elections in the United States. Much planetary emigration was taking place. The Pope declared the immaculate conception to be an article of faith. The Virgin Mary, meanwhile, was spotted in Lourdes a few years later. Aquariums were the latest in attractions and scientific research increased. Suez Canal construction was initiated; Atlantic Ocean travel accelerated. Witch trials were underway two waves before the one now being considered.

The Age of Aquarius, if not completely inaugurated with all that has come before, looms on the horizon. At this shift from Pisces to Aries waves, tension and mistrust will exist between North and South (or developed and Third World countries). The United Nations is going to be a tough organization to hold together, just as the U.S. was split apart by the Civil War. Such actions fit to a tee the Arian penchant for conflict.

Aries represents contrasts and opposition. Confrontation exhibits itself as rules are broken and limits tested. The basis for this is the principle of the matters at hand. Individual rights lay at the foundation of this sign. But winning at all costs is supreme in the mind, without a second thought about the consequences. That does not bode well for this time frame.

From 2024 to 2031 the Sun's negative force prevails. Egotism, pomposity, arrogance, and condescension will be the qualities foremost in the attitudes and actions of leaders all over the world. Heads of state are going to lead the way toward international conflict. Fathers, teachers, and older friends are the key personalities of this era.

More negative influences are to come. The Moon stands at center stage. Its impact is going to concentrate upon the emotions, sensitivity, and all liquids on Planet Earth. (It is known that the human body is 70 percent water, as is the entire global surface.) In addition, femininity, maternal instincts, and the family appear to be at the top of the totem pole of societies by past evidence. Light and dark (or day and night) correspond to daily rhythms that the Moon regulates to some degree, so look for these to be upset. Beyond that, death and changeability will be prominent in the seven years of its dominance.

Again history points to the end of the Civil War, followed by reconstruction with its immense corruption and indebtedness. (A repeat of this period implies that the developed nations will "win" the battle, only to "lose" the war.) The slaves were freed to a new dependence. A tremendous debt burden would no doubt translate into the need to create another economic system where everyone started from scratch. Hostilities were rampant on most parts of the planet in the mid- to late-nineteenth century. Tennessee became the home of the Ku Klux Klan, while the Salvation Army arose out of the Christian revivalism movement. The First Vatican Council announced papal infallibility. Interestingly enough, the premier book on eugenics was published. (Could *Star Trek* be right once more in accurately foreseeing a eugenics war?)

Going beyond the destruction, there most certainly will be a restructuring of the planet into a federation of sorts. One hundred years after the signing of the Universal Declaration of Human Rights (2048), a renewal of both legal and economic rights is going to take shape. It's likely to be initiated at that time. But it will evolve over a long period before actually functioning in a manner appropriate for the new mind-set of those remaining inhabitants. Just as the 1950s and 1960s proved to be a crucial time for isolated individuals to become an integral part of the larger society, history is going to parallel itself on a global scale.

Approaching the twenty-second century, critical deterioration of the ozone layer will have continued. Besides underwater cities, glass- or plastic-enclosed land communities are going to be required. Food supplies, too, will be victim of the enormous calamity. The survivors on Planet Earth then must pick up the pieces and combine their energies to step forward.

(As one of several lesser-developed beings, the human family has caused numerous disruptions. Immature people built their living areas and conducted business with minimal regard to plants, animals, and other life forms on the planet. In a parallel manner, some extraterrestrial visitors have apparently conducted examinations on human abductees with that same lack of compassion. In these instances, however, they simply present psychological and emotional obstacles with which to come to terms.

On Earth people have been a causative agent in extinctions of certain species of plants and animals. Larger elimination of tremendous numbers of life forms were evident in the past as the driving forces of the developing planet took form. At no time did this result in the eradication of all life all over the globe. And it never will! Humanity may destroy itself by ruining its own viable environment, but the entire Earth will go on an alternative path of that growth. The potential of the human species makes this possibility a very unlikely one.)

Chapter 5

The New Explorers

Every man and woman can expand his or her
own horizons via a combination of science and
metascience. This scenario is plain to see from the
historical records as events have unfolded. The
evolution of human life began with nature's technology (stones, water, and so forth), moving forward to manipulate nature by the brain (high
technology), then ending in the total use of mental
or psychic abilities. At present, high-tech machinery must and will be the vehicle to propel humanity
toward exclusive use of the mind sciences.

Aquarian Characteristics

The Age of Aquarius has been predicted to begin
anywhere from 2000 to 2150 to 12,000 A.D. How
will this era differ from the current one? A millennium of sorts is going to exist, with respect for
diversity and human cooperation becoming a reality. It will not be Utopia.

As an air sign, intelligence is the key for Aquarius. Through the challenges of the last age, the emotional nature of human existence will have been mastered to a large degree. People and nations will interact with the conscious recognition that the differences between all persons lends to universal growth and development. No one group or individual will have all the solutions to problems or know the best way to live. Cultural diversity will produce unique perspectives and provide a variety of views that assist in resolving issues.

Aquarius is concerned with group objectives. It will be a time of collective pursuits toward common goals of reform that reflect humanitarian and idealistic interests as highest priorities. A balance between freedom or independence of the individual and responsibility to the whole must be the central inner battle.

Progressiveness plus originality will be important characteristics. The mind's various faculties will be applied to studies of old and new subjects, bringing forth innovative information previously unknown. Some radical advancements constantly will come onto the scene. Intuition will be readily used in all professions, as it will be seen as a legitimate skill of decision-making capabilities. Eccentricity will become more visible as well.

Philosophical approaches to life circumstances will predominate. Whether it is called destiny or fate, events in one's day or at the workplace will not be seen as good or bad but simply as part of a learning process. This will eliminate past immature responses to what had been thought to be a negative experience. Rage or upsetting behavior is going to be a lot less likely.

The tone of the time period will exude a refined, pleasant, and generous atmosphere. Interpersonal relations between men and women will be such that platonic friendships will be the norm. This will permit the human family to understand gender issues in a more adult fashion in order to liberate both sexes from worn-out preconceptions. The same can be said of race, religion, and other stereotypical concepts.

Intimate relations will change. Love will take on a brotherly and sisterly, almost detached emotional appearance. Families are going to be smaller as women (especially) expand their achievements. Communal living arrangements will stand out, exemplifying the Keristan (San Francisco) practices. In this modality men and women continually will share in the experiences of a different partner. They aim to eliminate all envy, jealousy, possessiveness, and so on that the culture of the twentieth century dealt with in stressing monogamy. Children will be raised in a group setting, having more than one father or mother.

Enormous advantages will be observed within this environment. People will grow to care about increased numbers of community members. The old and infirmed will have many individuals around them who always will be there in time of need. Interdependence breeds involvement and leads to people able to effectively take control of their own lives.

Combining the visionary with the unconventional dictates that the Age of Aquarius is going to be highly inventive. New communication networks and novel computers will be operating. The mechanical aspects of science and business will prevail. Air and space breakthroughs suggest an enlarged space station, Moon base, Mars settlements, and solar system exploration in that order.

Such movement to the neighboring planets will parallel the human curiosity about what lies beyond our own immediate borders. Just as the land masses and ocean bodies were crossed centuries ago, the vastness of space presents humanity with a fresh challenge: other new worlds. Driven by the need to find a place for a growing population, raw materials, and the secrets of the cosmos, it looms so close but so far away. However, the resources required for this journey mandate that it must be performed by a united front.

In earlier epochs navigators sailed to nearby continents. Expanded voyages led to unknown lands. Colonization followed. Sea lanes were mapped along with landscape terrain. As the majority of continents had been examined, underwater surveys began. Inquiries into deeper and deeper realms of the ocean bottom are being financed to this day. This points to another clue to the end of the Piscean Age: the total investigation of the sea floor's contents.

Through these visits to other spinning globes in this system, there will be finds similar to those on Earth. Strange and unusual minerals, plants, and animals are going to be discovered. Eventually, when human consciousness is prepared for it, intelligent life forms (humanoid and completely different beings) will cross paths with one another. Extreme disparities may very well lead to primitive earthly reactions.

Space travel is destined to change with technology, reflecting modes used for land and sea penetration. This transportation evolution moved from human carriers to beast of burden to boat to balloon to car to airplane to rocket. Manufacturing typically starts small at individual levels, then huge plants with thousands of workers take over. The same will apply to space vehicles. Individual nations or companies initiated their construction. Shipyards are built near the water, so starships will be erected among the stars (in planetary orbit away from gravity's restraint). Propulsion systems will shorten trips via innovations that overcome what were thought to be limitations in previous centuries.

Along with these strides in transportation from place to place, inventions are going to constantly improve living and working conditions. This also is demonstrated by the evolution of the two-rigger into an ocean liner, a tent transformed by truck motorization into a luxurious motor home, and the single-person diving suit metamorphosed into a submarine. Future spacecraft undoubtedly will advance beyond the shuttle and primitive space station designs of the present. Already on the drawing boards are self-sufficient manufacturing facilities and biospheres containing agricultural capabilities. Merging these structures with fuel-driven vehicles produces the *Starship Enterprise* with all of its accoutrements.

Ways of making anything from technologies to materials to foods will proceed into the realm of increasing diversity. The human players themselves are going to be more cooperative and open to new ideas. They *must* be if the species is to go into the darkness of the cosmos. Problems will remain centered upon how to appropriately use technology. (Does one tamper with the ultimate arena of space and time, for example?) With the monstrous complexity of the technology, disasters could affect entire solar systems rather than a single planet.

The key to this exploration again reflects the Aquarian characteristic of intelligence. Moving out into the far reaches of the unknown requires enormous inner strength. Fear can no longer be paramount in the minds of the crew members. What better way to add comfort and safety than through a collective pursuit of this extraordinary frontier?

Expansion of the human family can be predicted to follow another pattern. As it extends its
boundaries further into the galaxies, a time will
come when it bumps up against other civilizations.
Repeating past errors with less drastic measures,
the growing settlements will infringe on their territories (as happened with Aborigines and American
Indian tribes). Some conflict is inevitable. With
intelligence as the dominant trait, those misunderstandings are going to be resolved with considerably less violence and ignorance.

Planet Earth will continue to participate in the
wonders of this age. Advances in many fields truly
may give this epoch a mystique of utopianism. As
responsibility and maturity have produced global
cooperation, problems will seem insignificant and
easily be attacked and conquered. Technological
improvements plus a guiding principle of preven-
tion as the basis for personal health and lifestyles
is sure to head off the creation of common illnesses
of the twentieth century. Gone are the television,
the radio, and other mechanisms of those days.

In an age of taking control of individual actions
through discipline and self-determination, a needs-
based system has replaced the old economics.
After all, consciously realizing that the human
family is one must translate into a society that
practices what it preaches. All peoples yearn to live
with human dignity, do what helps their personal
growth in their own way, and have the necessary
materials to develop mentally and physically to the
fullest.

Mental abilities translate into more than mere
scientific and technological inventiveness. Devices,
whether machines or drugs, are tools that can be
used to allow humanity to go forward in its own
evolution. During the 2000 years that has unfolded, a proliferation of mind capabilities will yield

functions of which the last century saw only a glimpse.

Bob Beck, a neuroscience researcher in Los Angeles, built what he terms a "brain tuner." This battery-operated contraption uses magnetic oscillations in the 7.8-hertz range to induce a vibrational change in the wearer's brain. He claims to have successfully done so in hundreds of subjects. Beck says that the tuner has caused altered states of consciousness, improved memory, drug addiction cures, as well as production of pain-killing endorphins in his experiments. (Some such devices are available through New Age mail order houses.)

Thousands of years from now there will be technologies that go far beyond these early attempts, following a natural progression of human development. First, outside gadgets are created to bring forth and assist growth. At a later point in time, no technology will be necessary as psychic man and woman become a reality.

Throughout history this planet has observed a small share of ordinary individuals of both genders who have revealed clues to the mind's potential. Some were figures such as Joan of Arc and Albert Einstein. Others grew to fame due to their selfless dedication to helping members of their communities throughout their lives (Edgar Cayce, Eileen Garrett, *et al.*). Extrasensory perception, or the sixth sense, is the term that has been associated with this mental capability. Extensive studies of this so-called phenomenon are clairvoyance, clairaudience, precognition, telepathy, and retrocognition. These and additional marvels of the mind relate directly to that which metaphysicians have referred to as the sixth kingdom of the etheric state of existence.

Clairvoyance has been dubbed "second sight."

It is the ability to pick up distant objects and events in the mind. Clairaudience relates to hearing sounds or voices that are equally far away. Precognition, on the other hand, permits someone to know in advance that an event will take place before it actually does. Retrocognition, conversely, pertains to receiving information or pictures mentally about an occurrence that already came to pass long ago. There's also telepathy, a mind-to-mind communication between people. (Identical twins are frequently able to perform such feats.)

Surveys, including Gallup polls, academic questionnaires of students and the general public, and random national samplings by numerous magazines, show that people accept the reality of some psychic phenomena. Recently, 67 percent of American adults said they believe that experiences like those just mentioned are real. Twenty million of those questioned also described personally profound paranormal episodes. University parapsychological research currently is being performed in the United States, Russia, France, Germany, the Netherlands, Japan, India, and Great Britain.

Traditional professions have been using the skills of psychics. Police agencies resort to assistance when they hit dead ends in murder or missing persons cases. Archaeologists bring them along to establish where to dig for artifacts of ancient civilizations. They even are consulted for the dating or identification of specific findings. (That information then is correlated with scientific knowledge.) Military sectors of various countries have experimented with placing thoughts into the minds of officials of opposing nations.

Scientific study of psychic phenomenon has revealed mixed results. There seem to be a small group of people who are consistently accurate in remote viewing or telepathy tests. "Remote viewing" is a term applied to clairvoyance. Subjects will sketch or describe the surroundings where a second person is located. Some trials have involved attempts to send and receive pictures from specially constructed cards. Even Apollo 17 astronaut Edgar Mitchell participated in an experiment similar to this during his Moon voyage in 1971.

These investigations have exceeded mere perceptual studies into the realm of the essence of life itself. Ganzfield rooms arose from a "whole field" theory of reality. Devised in 1971, this concept was built around the idea that psychic phenomena are most prolific in the dream state. A subject's eyes are covered completely, his or her ears are filled with white noise (hiss of an untuned TV station) via headphones, and the room is kept perfectly quiet and bathed in red light. This approach allows the participant to focus on inner images. A variation of this--the relaxation tank, which permits the user to unwind while floating inside--has been put into commercial use.

Dreams, too, are a part of this research. It is known that American Indians would start their day by meeting to discuss members' experiences the night before. The symbology would be unraveled by the chief or medicine man so that each person could get off to an insightful daily adventure. Other cultures performed similar rituals.

Currently, findings from this field of endeavor show fascinating effects. There generally are four or five separate dream periods lasting approximately ten minutes each. The brain remains alert although the individual is hard to rouse. The frequency of the brain waves in this state matches that of channeling.

Psychokinesis is another form of psi power. With mental concentration a few individuals have succeeded in altering physical environments. This included changing the air temperature in a room and a sealed vacuum bottle. Uri Geller is perhaps the best-known metal spoon bender, although he is not the only one. In addition, various people have demonstrated the ability to move objects without touching them.

Extrasensory perception is considered unnatural by some, but the term fits perfectly with what it entails. The term means to go beyond the limitations of the five senses (feeling, sight, taste, hearing, and smell). Animal and bird populations can hear sounds at very low frequencies that are undetectable by the human ear. Slowly, sensory navigation is being understood by those studying it. Marine animals speak to one another via sound underwater. Schools of fish move and alter their directions simultaneously via signals from within the group. Bats also maneuver employing sound as a guide.

Three basic theories exist to explain psychic abilities. All of these phenomena seem to contradict accepted laws of the physical world. It is thought that established sensory channels are the only ones. The speed of light is considered the upper limit at which energy (information) can travel. ESP prods those in the here and now to wonder if the present knowledge available is definitive or absolute. (Of course it isn't. This is not a perfect world.)

One idea concerns invisible waves that have extremely low frequencies. A second talks about the psi dimension outside of but interconnected with the physical human environment. The third revolves around quantum mechanics, describing a total interplay of everything that makes up the cosmos at the subatomic level.

Even the ages-old practice of dowsing fits into

this equation. Individuals who can find water without digging for it have existed since time immemorial. They place a Y-shaped twig or metal rods between their thumb and fingers. At a site where the well location is to be drilled, they walk the land until the twig bends downward or the rods cross. Another ability in this line of work centers on the use of a pendulum placed over a map of the area until the pendulum stops swinging.

Electromagnetic fields were thought to be the basis for dowsing. However, when a person's body cannot interact with a geologic substructure (where the water supply sits), this theory has been put on the shelf. The example of the map dowser puzzles researchers to this day.

Finally, there is the matter of Kirlian photography. An argument from the metaphysicians says that it proves that auras are real. Processed film portrays a halo of varying colors around the living tissue of a hand, leaves, and flower petals. Stranger still are the Kirlian images of cut leaves showing an energy matrix outlining the portion removed. (People relate feelings of phantom pain in a limb that has been amputated.)

Morphology is the study of why matter takes on a particular shape. Inquiries into this subject lead back to energy matrices. The best information comes from Yale University, where Burr made a detailed investigation. His discoveries demonstrated that electromagnetic fields encompass and permeate all life forms from their earliest stages. In fact, they order and control the physical matter that comprises a certain plant, animal, or human body. In other words the field is preset so that the cells expand to fit an invisible mold.

What all of this information reveals becomes quite obvious. The human world is truly interconnected with all life at a cosmic scale. The numerous correlations provided by this author are amazingly harmonizing. The implications for the next stage of existence follow on the heals of these astounding revelations.

Etheric states reflect a reversal of the Adam and Eve process of gaining self-awareness. The new semiphysical life forms separate from exclusive connection to Planet Earth and return to their inclusion with the entirety of space and time. In this transformation The All expresses itself through one additional vehicle; the sixth root race of the human family is near at hand.

Prior to their arrival, the inhabitants of Earth must begin and then expand what has been called the sixth sense. People who increasingly exhibit clairvoyance, clairaudience, telepathy, precognition, plus all additional powers could become the new witches. In a civilization where intelligence prevails, it is unlikely that the panic and witch hunts of former centuries will reoccur. However, a period of adjustment may be necessary for some.

As increasing numbers of individuals possess these abilities, societies will develop different quandaries about their impact on everyday life. Ethical questions, especially, are going to predominate the scene and stretch present imaginations. Does someone who knows the future advise a soon-to-be space voyager that this is his or her last journey? What about entire crews? And should major or minor injuries be foretold?

There are added things to ponder. If a meteor is to strike a certain planet, will evacuation plans be implemented and how many inhabitants will believe it? Do laziness and physical decline arise from using psychokinesis instead of manual labor? Can mere intuition or ESP be the sole basis for decision-making when many lives depend upon those steps to be taken?

With a widening emphasis placed on the mind sciences, something is going to be lost as this development proceeds. This is exemplified by people who put most of their personal energies into nonhuman-oriented activities. They lose the ability to love or have compassion for others. Empathy disappears. Professionals who get wrapped up in their work, whether it's a scientific research project or the corporate game of acquiring power, represent such examples.

Knowledge for knowledge's sake can take on an overriding preoccupation. UFO abductees espouse this exact mind-set as a characteristic of their examiners. When brought aboard for scrutiny they are treated as specimens (in much the same way that scientists treat subjects in the laboratory). Another allegation made by those abductees relates to the extraterrestrial visitors' comments that (in a few cases) indicate their civilization is on the ropes due to the fact they have ceased to be able to nurture their young. (In other words, they're dying.)

Learning will continue as the evolutionary process unfolds. Other changes in attitudes and priorities are going to become plain. As the physical and emotional natures of life are conquered, the mental aspect remains.

The human family has reached a point of advancement where intelligence is the major trait. Responsible and mature applications are the next challenge. Will these newly found powers be too tempting? To some, yes. As the need for technology dwindles, a replay of former crises looms on the horizon.

In a previous epoch conflict arose between those creating and using the technologies, and others not able to afford them. Now there are the possessors of mind-stretching capabilities versus the population in which they have yet to develop.

Will knowledge again override wisdom? Absolutely not! Minor clashes may surface. The ultimate test, though, is yet to come.

Struggles existed in the distant past to control manmade weaponry. As the Age of Capricorn beckons, the mental battleground awaits. The time frame will be late in the fortieth century. A majority of individuals have fully developed psi powers. It comes down to the responsible and the mature against those who cannot master their omnipotent faculties. Who will prevail?

While the Aquarian influence is still in effect, the outcome is clear. The group cohesiveness of civilization insures that those able to exercise the power of thought energies wisely are going to triumph during the showdown of the "Battle of the Gods." The determination of life and death now is available to Earth's latest product: etheric beings. Successfully meeting this final human challenge, the fifth kingdom is reached. Evolutionary development stands on the threshold between total material existence and complete invisibility.

Beyond Technology

This dualist search for truth through outer (space) and inner (mind) resources eventually will eliminate technology as a necessary vehicle for continued human development. Energy and matter are interchangeable. The brain possesses ongoing operations involving electrochemical signals racing through it. Thoughts are merely energy forms. The progression to mind transformations, where thoughts become the reality, must be the next stage in human evolution.

A fresh start will begin when this ultimate crisis of mind has been overcome. Space and time will be the new playground of what humanity has become.

Along with the wise use of this enormous power must come an understanding that no one should interrupt the process of universal growth and development. Each and every life form has to be allowed to undertake its own evolution in its own way. Noninterference is the one universal law that will be respected at this level of consciousness.

When advancement moves forward to the astral state, a new step is going to have been made up the ladder of evolution. It is one of total invisibility that separates life from the material Earth to the infinity of timeless space. Perfection is still an elusive quality. Immense wisdom and enlightenment are held within these beings, who are gaining a one-ness with The All. They have another level of maturity to acquire. Some are pranksters while others can leave well enough alone at lesser states of existence.

The astral realm has been called the home of the angels. Throughout history there have been stories preserved in ancient writings about meetings and communications with unearthly entities of light. Photographs and personal experiences with ghostly figures add to these stories. In more recent times there have been reports of nonphysical beings arriving in spaceships.

Another aspect of this featureless arena re-volves around the idea of astral travel. It concerns an enduring belief that a part of the self can journey outside of the body. Some label this the spirit or soul, while others use such esoteric terms as "monad" or "essence."

Philosophies and religious teachings present a common belief that the spirit and body exist apart from each other. It is written that one dies and the second lives on. Reincarnation has been suggested as a sort of cosmic recycling. Supplementary con-siderations talk about the soul either reaping a reward or being punished in a heaven or hell, respectively. Universally these portray similar concepts.

Over 78,000,000 people on Planet Earth say they have participated in some kind of nonphysical excursion beyond the physical body. Spiritual voyages typically are of three variations. First, there is the out-of-the-body experience, or OBE. Individuals speak of visiting distant relatives and recognizing the surroundings, or seeing familiar faces while not being seen by anyone around them. Shirley MacLaine, for one, has even described traveling off of the globe into the far reaches of space.

OBEs have been recorded since the beginning of history. Many people in various cultures wrote about these happenings. Studies reveal that no race, ethnic group, or national group stands out above others in recounting the phenomenon. Occupation also seems to be irrelevant to the OBEr. It is estimated that one out of every 100 persons undergoes such an experience sometime during his or her life.

Investigators in this field refer to these occurrences as archetypal--available to all members of the human family. The ancient Egyptians said that their "ba" departed the body and hovered above it. The Germans spoke of their "doppelganger." "Vardger" was the word in Norway. Scottish peoples told tales of the "taslach." "Fetch" comes from the Old English literature.

The story of the Greek Hermotimus of Clazomene portrays a constant travel in the astral realm. His wife grew tired of him always being "out of town," so she asked his friends to watch over his body while she went out for the day. They burned the body, leaving his soul to wander aimlessly. Even Elisha, of Old Testament fame, was able to eavesdrop on a hostile Syrian king so as to obtain the needed information that would insure an Israelite victory.

The example of American Sylvan Joseph Muldoon is atypical but deserves mention. In a book published in 1929, he spoke of his OBE when he was 12 years old. Muldoon awoke suddenly. He felt rigid and immobile. Then his astral body began vibrating rapidly in an up-and-down motion. There was extreme pressure in the back of his head. Muldoon realized in a split second that he now could hear and see. But he noticed he was floating above his bed. The two bodies were said to be connected by an elastic cable. He returned later with a jerk of the cord from his physical self lying in its bed after short trips around a camp where he was staying.

Scientific studies centered on this topic have collected thousands of firsthand accounts of individuals going through out-of-the-body experiences. Separation occurs at the hands and feet, with the final exit at the head. Many report clicking or a blackout just prior to parting as a customary event. Discomfort and fear apparently are not normal feelings. In addition, brain waves in test subjects show that they are indeed not in a deep sleep or dream state when the OBE takes place.

Animal experiments in this arena provide more food for thought. Kittens were put in an isolated room a few miles from the person trying to achieve an OBE. The cats' actions were noted before and after visitation attempts to the room were made. On the occasions when the experience was successful (according to the subjects), the active kittens would sit down quietly. The opposite happened with the use of a snake. The reptile rose up and struck out at something during the out-of-the-body endeavors.

Near-death experiences are an additional form of astral travel. Those having gone through it claim that it occurred in a number of instances and under varying circumstances. Patients undergoing surgery have spoken of a floating of some part of the self above the operating table, watching everything that was being performed. (They later told nurses or doctors specific procedures that they performed.) In actual cases of death, where brain and heart activity cease, individuals characterize their experience as one in which they are approaching a light at the end of an infinitely long tunnel. Along the way they meet relatives or friends who have passed away. A feeling of ecstasy and an urge to complete the journey overcome them before returning to their bodies.

The effects of an out-of-the-body experience generally are profound. Many people alter their lifestyles. They renew their values and beliefs. Expressions regarding life after death and worlds beyond the senses are a part of the transformation. Exactly what is all of this revealing about the astral state?

A dimension of nonphysical boundaries opens unlimited doors to every creature who has earned its wings for the endless flight into the spiritual world. Energies of unimaginable power lay in wait for their application to the completion of the cosmos.

The sixth stage of evolution prevails in this realm. It is the state where spirit or energy beings take on the challenge of spiritual attunement. Just as humanity is composed of children, adolescents, adults, and adepts, so is the invisible universe.

Children begin life by learning the conventions of society. They must learn to coordinate their body functions. Their minds have to be filled with information that in turn can assist the individual with his or her personal growth. Another factor is that of cultural relativism that structures knowledge within a certain framework of a paradigm handed down from generation to generation.

In an expanse without physical needs or concerns, learning to use spiritual or energy bodies creates demands greater than that associated with the human realm. Since this life is based on what could be considered universal powers, "children and adolescents" must master various kinds of thought-energy on a cosmic scale. As "adults" they are required to apply those energies for the perfection of the cosmos in any number of "professions." The wiser elements of the astral dimension take on larger and increasingly complex operations. So-called "adepts" perform those functions that hold the cosmos together. (These relate to the interconnections of solar systems, galaxies, and so on.)

All of this may sound extremely esoteric. But with a universal perspective it fits the picture perfectly. Earthly children are taught the essential basics of what they must know to live in a society. A sense of self, language, arithmetic, reading, physical coordination, and so forth are useful in this task. Adolescents move on to slightly more advanced lessons, as an awareness of social interactions intensifies. Adults are expected to utilize the knowledge in their jobs. As they do, wisdom develops in certain areas and leads to expertise. The wiser individuals then have the opportunity to take on leadership, counseling, or consulting positions. At the top rung of civilization, those coordinating the planetary activities join forces that go beyond nationalistic objectives. (The United Nations is the closest organization to date expressing these ideals.)

Astral residents range in scope from single entities to group beings. This latter designation reflects the collective orientation of human workers in scientific research laboratories, assembly line employees in industry, and think tanks that turn out detailed reports for the long-term future. Teams of individuals are required to invent, construct, and test the final products created. This, too, will take place in the invisible state of being. Specialists and multidisciplinarians are additional members of this unique world.

Energy forms also devour food. It's not food of the physical kind or of the earthly variety. It is energy in all of its infinite categories. (After all, meals possess energy for physical needs.) Black holes have been observed absorbing light from their surroundings. Technological discoveries through the years unveiled X-rays, electromagnetic radiation, and countless waves or pulses of energy. There are a multitude available to the astral beings. What is not consumed is applied to cosmic construction.

Simple human life forms could not begin to imagine the wonders awaiting them as they traverse space and then time. Due to limitations that are a part of the human condition, these treasures remain hidden. As understanding and growth propel the human family into the unknown, the universe will continue to be a university of broad and expanding scope. Responsibilities must grow equally as well.

Finally, as the spiritual essence reaches complete perfection, the causal state reunites that essence with The All. The circle of growth is coming to an end. As all life expressions conclude their own evolution, The All becomes perfect via the infinite diversity It has experienced. Universes, galaxies, stars, and planets, plus the components contained on each spinning body, fulfill their specific destinies. As each returns to the source from which they have come, The All adds to Its own genetic cosmic makeup, permitting It to create new elements throughout the vastness of space.

A description of this arena is extremely difficult to put into words. Inhabitants aim toward pure consciousness at the highest pinnacle of this state. In an elementary sense the grand designers of the cosmos are carrying out their work. The ultimate coordinators of every action being taken at the astral stage exist in this plane. Other "occupations" involve star building, architects of the universes, as well as those preparing to finalize their knowledge of the big picture in all its detail.

No matter the level of existence in which one finds him or her self, challenges are the key to growth. Whether it is at the microscopic or macroscopic frame of reference, overcoming obstacles brings forth untold rewards. For men and women on Planet Earth, the future holds inconceivable riches that go far beyond mere material wealth.

Chapter 6

The Ultimate Challenge

People everywhere may continue to argue over who is right and what religion or philosophy belongs to the one "God." However, all members of the human family remain imperfect and constrained in their knowledge of absolute truth. It is purely egotism that impels individuals to profess that they have that one truth. Even if they did, as Christ found out, not everyone has yet evolved to the point where they are able to comprehend it. A fixed set of parochial principles has replaced personal growth through betterment, and that improvement can take place in diverse ways.

Reincarnation as a belief has been around for thousands of years. Its theme proclaims that a cosmic recycling of the human spirit or soul follows death. Certainly all of the wisdom to be acquired, plus the mastery of the self, must take longer than a single life span of 40 to 100 years. A continuous return to the Earth can be the only answer.

Ancient Egyptians included texts that attested to the virtues of the individual in his or her coffin so that the god Osiris would grant the deceased further lives. Reincarnation is suspected of being a belief in Stone Age civilizations dating back 13,000 years ago. Archaeologists have unearthed bodies from that period buried in the fetal position. This indicates a preparation for a literal rebirth of the spirit.

Christian theologians regard such talk with disdain. What few realize is that reincarnation was espoused by priests going all the way back to the time Christ's teaching were widely distributed. One such follower, Origen of Alexandria, had his writings condemned by Pope Anastasius in 400 A.D. However, those writings continued to be prominent until the thirteenth century. Recent polls show that nearly one-quarter of Americans, Britons, French, and West Germans accept the legitimacy of spiritual rebirth.

Studies of past lives have been underway for a couple of decades. Through hypnosis clinicians are able to regress ordinary people back past their births to another period in history. Researchers have identified this method as one of three possible ways people are able to recount previous existences.

A second method, spontaneous recollection, occurs most commonly in children. Many seem to have experiences in which they remember, without prompting, a prior life. This is the largest generator of evidence regarding reincarnation. Dreams figure prominently here, as individuals either receive messages or pregnant women meet former relatives who are no longer alive. In this latter case the mother-to-be is told that she will give birth to that ancestor in its new form.

Traumatic accidents stimulate recall of a past life. Sojourns to locations that were connected to a previous incarnation can trigger this feeling. Déja vu has been widely associated with reincarnation as well. When a momentary sensation in which a consciously unfamiliar scene or event brings forth this response, a deeply stored thought is propelled to the surface. Children have proven to be the best examples because of their short number of life experiences.

Add to this the phenomenon of cryptomenesia. People have related detailed bits of information while in a hypnotic trance that they cannot recall in a regular state of wakefulness. Then there is xenoglossia, a demonstration of the ability to speak a foreign language only in that same state. In many instances of past life regression, whatever its form, historical searches accurately have confirmed languages spoken, personal identities ascribed, plus details few people could know.

In psychology studies there seem to be people who are possessed or suffer from multiple personalities. Psychotics also describe additional states of reality in which their hallucinations (other beings) exist. Both of these examples, in part, along with those knowing of a past life, demonstrate the idea of a more-complicated universe than is presently thought to subsist. For reasons of sanity those other personalities must remain submerged so that the current one can move forward along the pathway of development. (Psychologists say that severe abuse of some kind triggers these multiple selves to come to the forefront.)

Superconsciousness, as Jung and his colleagues labeled it, joins the mind/brain to the cosmos in its entirety. All of the seemingly unrelated material in this book points out that much rethinking is necessary. Yet if one contemplates in universal terms what the ancient philosophers were stating, one sees that they were revealing that everything is interlinked. The only difference is that they used words and concepts related to their specific cultures and knowledge base.

The Wheel of Becoming from Tibetan Buddhism depicts the cycle of death and rebirth. On the way to enlightenment, it speaks of 49 days between lives. Gender changes are a normal part of the process, as individuals who have been regressed recount. This matches the beliefs of the Burmese and Kutchin Indians of Canada. (One researcher, who established 250 cases, found that even birthmarks and scars recur on the same spot.) The practice is celebrated by the Balinese, Hindu, Druse, Tlingit Indians of Alaska, and other cultures.

In the late-twentieth century, fresh approaches to old spiritual teachings must center on the commonalities among all of the separate fields of study. That can move civilization through this extremely critical time frame by bringing people together. Combining these ideas with the secular world and its operations will produce a new paradigm that can carry humanity toward its destiny.

Dogmatically structured religions turn former believers away. With individuality so strong, no set of strict rules by which to live is going to allow fulfillment for everyone. The dogma fails when its importance is diminished or it is perceived to be irrelevant in modern times. Rituals must come alive and the symbology used has to be clearly understood.

The cult phenomenon came onto the scene to a large degree because of this issue. Cults offered a renewed sense of awe to a very technologically oriented civilization. They also exuded love, sharing, a feeling of community or family, stability, and structure. There's always bad with the good, and many cults produced dictatorial control of their members, brainwashing, drug and personal abuse, corruption of the values they openly embraced, coercion, and mass suicide.

The search for truth goes forward. When one route ends, another path always is available. In every society a pinnacle is reached. It is a challenge to the human family to recognize and constantly transform past ideas into applications for an ever-changing vision of how the cosmos works and humanity's place in it. Absent of replenishment, decline sets in as history lays out before its readers.

Looking for outside saviors to suddenly create a perfect world is simplistic and immature. Whether it is a superhuman, god-man, or visitors from a neighboring galaxy, men and women are on their own. Cooperation through growth and development is all the stimulus the human family needs as time unfolds. The infancy of Planet Earth has to conclude soon. Those ready to grow up will; eventually, all children must.

Responsibility goes hand in hand with maturity. All change begins at an individual level. That can occur only with the proper guidelines. Fresh answers to deep, burning questions can assist that development. Using the paradigm laid out here within a context of a totally integrated cosmos, those issues easily are comprehended.

Each person is at a unique point in his or her individual evolution. It can be measured in terms of either human or spirit age. The spiritual life experiences are the key. Therefore, no single philosophical, religious, social, political, or economic system can fit every culture or be appropriate for all people. A general framework that emphasizes the theme of personal maturity is the starting place.

Command of one's life must take center stage within this perspective. Lacking self-mastery, control of outer resources or environments is an illusion. All the money and power in the world temporarily can guarantee domination. Groups of individuals will only take so much before they revolt. Material objects and devices fail for unknown reasons. Even the Earth has shown that it will sustain but a certain amount of pollution or mishandling. Then it, too, erupts.

Seven Deadly Sins

The real obstacles reside inside each person. Envy, pride, lust, anger, covetousness, gluttony, and sloth are called the seven deadly sins (there's that number again!). What they reveal about an individual's state of development provides clues to what qualities must be mastered.

Pride refers to an undue sense of one's own superiority. Since all people are unique in their own developmental process, it is impossible to say that some are better than others. Many individuals may know a lot of pieces of information. There are surely those who are stronger physically. But human beings never will be perfect. Acceptance of one another is the key to overriding this mind-set.

Envy is defined as a feeling of resentment or discontent over another's attainments, endowments, or possessions. As stated above, no one is better than anyone else. Each person has the innate ability to perform outstandingly in their fields of interest. It takes hard work and commitment to achieve the goals that one sets. Then again, some societies measure success and emphasize material wealth as their highest priorities. The inner qualities are the characteristics that make for true prosperity.

Lust concerns excessive sexual desires. This runs the gamut from pleasure-seeking, wanting to fulfill a drive, to wanting to control others' affections for selfish purposes. The individual who falls into this trap permits the drive to dominate him or her. Thinking that all men or women will be attracted to a single person is an extremely egotistical view. Self-love is the important place to start, but without the ego as the predominant aspect that puts someone in the center of things.

Anger relates to a feeling of sudden, strong displeasure and antagonism directed against the cause of an assumed wrong or injury. In every case the emotion arises from within the individual. It is a response to another's remark or action that brings to mind a weakness or frailty, which no one likes to admit. Perceptions of hopelessness lead to eruptions of anger. Things that no single person has control over also will tend to jar a release of temper. Just remember that no one and nothing can make any member of the human family mad.

Covetousness or greediness is the state of being overly desirous of things, usually of a material nature. It could pertain to money, possessions, or family members (wife, children) belonging to another. These generally are used to displace inner needs. A reorientation is necessary--one must look inward to determine what qualities remain undeveloped.

Gluttony, or the habit of eating or doing other things to excess, follows from the previous deadly sin. This lifestyle develops over a long period of time and continually is reinforced; it is living without thinking. Many behavioral studies of obese people show that they eat more than they should because of loneliness. Others seem to possess a chemical imbalance in certain brain functions, which the food activates. (Could this deficiency develop over many lifetimes, impressed upon the genetic composition of the spirit?)

Last but not least, there is sloth, a disinclination to exertion that can mean several different things. It relates to a lack of wanting to exercise. Beyond that individuals would rather go through life without obstacles to surmount or challenges to meet. It's easier to avoid taxing physical, mental, or spiritual demands, even if they're for maintenance or health reasons. This, too, is a childish way to approach living. Without determining individual limits and pushing beyond them, growth cannot occur. (Look at the great scientific or historical breakthroughs.)

When seen in this light, real personal and then societal progress can be made through an inner-directed philosophy of improvement. The human family, encouraged toward self-betterment, will transform civilization from a material-centered emphasis to a balanced system of unending development. Along this journey additional concepts must be considered in a fresh way.

It has been said that there is a specific road to travel or means to achieve enlightenment. With the infinite diversity of the cosmos reflected through humanity, it becomes obvious that that statement is untrue. In general terms guidelines have been laid out for everyone to follow using universal ideals. They would prevent or minimize the chance of power or influence falling into the hands of a few people. (Power corrupts and absolute power corrupts absolutely.)

The time has come for each individual to take those necessary steps that can be made only by personal commitment. No longer is it practical to have leaders who tell their followers how to act or treat one another. Waiting for others to take the bull by the horns is irresponsible behavior. Many authorities in recent years (and throughout history) let down their people either due to hypocrisy (do as I say, not as I do) or corruption of the system for selfish material gain.

Destiny Versus Free Will

An age-old debate has ensued over how destiny and free will relate to each other in the overall scheme of things. Recent events at the local community or global level really make one wonder about these two important, seemingly esoteric ideas.

Free will is simply the ability to think and act for one's self, using the limited knowledge all individuals possess. Personal and social problems take shape because people go about their daily routines, driven by inner- and outer-directed wants and desires. Some apply religious teachings or philosophies that they have been exposed to since birth. Another segment of the population has adapted to what they have learned through interactions with others around them since early life, and in observing what the larger society emphasizes.

In this way ideals become altered to accommodate the real world of imperfect beings. Those few who do hold to the absolutes find it impossible to participate in the mainstream. Many try to force their expectations, derived from the teachings, upon the rest of society. Others drop out into the comfort of their immediate family, forming a community to preserve the ideals.

Problems are created when stereotypes and preconceptions arise from oversimplifying complicated ideas contained in any highly developed universal discourse. The less complex an individual is in his or her makeup, the easier it is to accept these notions. It takes no effort to believe that all blacks or Jews have peculiar qualities that set them apart from others. And yet they have the same essential physiology and the same needs as all other human beings. Within each group or nationality, individuals exist that are as different as the stars composing the heavens.

Narrow perspectives about how the cosmos functions and our place in the big picture also leads to preconceptions. If one does not understand the unfolding historical record and how the various belief systems have arisen, ridicule of others due to particular religious practices proves ignorance. Fear also is a very real part of this issue. There are those who think that exposure to alien ideas will change their accepted beliefs and entice them to commit strange and terrible acts.

The core of this subject is the unknown. It is a very deeply rooted aspect that goes back to ancient times. The human psyche acquired this from its earliest years in an environment of unexplainable marvels. In strengthening the inner qualities of each individual, this immature view of life and one another will vanish. Nothing is to be feared--except the human reaction to give in to it.

Every action that is undertaken by the individual is therefore an expression of free will. Bad things happen because of irresponsibility or ignorance. Living in an imperfect world dictates that accidents will occur. Injury or death is a reality of interactions on Planet Earth. Sometimes it is intentional while on other occasions it is not.

Plane, train, or automobile crashes are a risk of our technological lifestyle. People hurry or do not pay full attention to their surroundings. Drivers, pilots, or engineers may be impaired by drugs or even a head cold. Repairs are performed by experts or novices with the same results. (Even experts have a bad day.) Unforeseen quirks in materials are far too often a very real part of the civilization as it exists today.

"Acts of God," one of the most misapplied ideas, has been a long-standing term used by insurance companies as well as government officials. Usually it refers to natural disasters such as flooding, volcanic activity, earthquakes, tornadoes, and so forth. There is still a prevalent mind-set that prescribes to a belief that the superior being has nothing better to do than sit around choosing who lives or dies, which wrecks occur and which do not, and other daily activities.

The reason this is absurd is that the basic universal process is one of growth and development. Learning only takes place when mistakes are made. (Otherwise this would be a utopia or paradise.) This also explains why a certain number of accidents must happen before improvements are instituted, and that includes everything from traffic lights to the latest safety equipment for nuclear power plants.

For more long-term changes to be introduced, an increase in consciousness (or deeper understanding of life) is required. Psychic phenomena are not yet accepted as being real by the majority of the global population. The concept of Earth as a finite ball in space was initiated with the pictures sent back from the Moon during the Apollo missions. The threats of pollution and destructive weapons gained a hold on human minds through their immense impact (perceived or actual) on everyday life (tainted food supplies, loss of species, negative health effects, and so on).

People working with their free will can do wonderful things within the appropriate guidelines (morals, values) or they can abuse themselves and those around them. But they must have a definite relationship to the social system in which they reside. As old, universal ideals are recognized to pertain to the technological world, many critical issues can be approached in fresh ways.

Even death as seen in this universal perspective

has changed. There are those who cannot comprehend how infants or children are "permitted" to die so young. If death is a final state, this surely is confusing. But it is not! The lesson learned at such an early age, that death is a change of state, carries through to the next existence. This is then one less idea for them to grapple with upon their return.

Helplessness is another concern. It is impossible to be in control of every situation at all times of the day. Watching and safeguarding children 24 hours a day, 365 days a year, simply is unrealistic. They will get into trouble. But that's learning. Injuries and deaths occur due to their ignorance or irresponsibility. Adults, in whom they place their trust, give in to inappropriate drives or immature actions.

Loved ones will be in accidents of their own doing or caused by others. Some could have been avoided while others were not. Computers declare people deceased. (Actually it's either the human operator or program created by the human operator that is the cause.) Terrorists hijack planes to other countries. On and on it goes. The world is not always fair in its treatment of the individual, but trying to place blame or inflict guilt simply compounds obstacles in the way of self-development.

Perhaps the greatest puzzlement that continues to haunt humanity is the Holocaust of World War II. Both survivors and outside observers ponder why it happened. Many still add to the equation the "God" factor. How could God let it go forth? This obscures the true picture.

The Holocaust can be portrayed simplistically by viewing it as Germans persecuting Jews, Catholics, and Gypsies. It was really human beings killing other human beings. The lessons of this extermination yet have not been fully learned. Since the Holocaust there have been similar events on various parts of the planet (Cambodia, Jonestown, and so forth). The possibility of future mass deaths remains until those lessons are impressed into the consciousness of every inhabitant of Planet Earth.

The slaughter of huge numbers of people occurs because large groups give up their capability to think to a leader figure. They follow orders without a second thought. Negative stereotypes of the victims are accepted as true. Charisma excites the emotions and hypnotizes the mind. Beliefs win out over knowledge. Institutions discourage questioning long-honored practices.

Modern-day business organizations and governmental bodies are arranged so that power and control increase as one climbs the ladder. This reflects the king, who as leader was closest to the all-knowing God. It also relates to the priest, still today regarded as God's representative on Earth. After all, is the individual worker or the church member as worthy or as able as the person at the top?

The point that needs to be made goes back to the fact that every person possesses a part of The All. The All knows everything because it is the source of all information and wisdom. A belief system reflects acceptance of the truth without proof that it is. Faith consists of trust in the institution or head of the organization who acts as the keeper of the truth. (Corruptible human beings are an ever-present possibility.) Managers and priests alike are trained rigorously and indoctrinated with dogmatic, inflexible information. Little attention is put into the inner qualities of those individuals.

Throughout many of the teachings of the numerous religions, people are socialized into accepting that they are incapable of thinking for themselves. (We are all sinners!) Each person grows to believe this is the reality. As a result there is hardly any incentive to try to improve. Some teachings merely reflect that all that is necessary is to recognize an ancient personality as their God or savior to win a place in a heavenly afterlife. This requires no transformation on the part of the individual in this life.

On the opposite front, many sects create strict daily routines that must be followed to the letter. The rules are so rigid that very little thinking is allowed. The entire purpose of these rituals, once again, is to secure a spot in some extraordinary kingdom. There are diverse numbers of additional beliefs somewhere in between this and the previously mentioned material. Even the social, political, and economic subsystems deter dissent or behavior out of the prescribed norm.

Charismatic personalities excite the emotional nature of the self. But when used to dominate rather than spur others' growth, their power is to be recognized for what it represents. In the Nazi era discussed here, many people looked up to Hitler as a god, just as the Italians glorified Mussolini and the Japanese worshipped Hirohito. These authorities could do no wrong--but the same applied to Pol Pot and Jim Jones. Of course, all of these leaders were merely human.

The moral of the story should be plain. True leaders encourage their followers to think for themselves. Wisdom is expressed through a process that stimulates the individual to develop and mature with minimal guidance and without dependence. In addition, self-control prevents the individual from being swayed by an outside force. This is the starting place for this awakening of consciousness.

The ultimate challenge to humanity in the late twentieth century centers upon transformation of their religious or philosophical beliefs into self-truth. But how can anyone "know" the truth? First, grasp the fact that new information is revealing that the ancients possessed an enlightened perspective. With so many correlating pieces of knowledge painting a portrait of the superconsciousness as outlined in this book, there now can be no doubts that everything is indeed interconnected with The All.

Turning inward is a second approach. Each person must embark on a multidisciplinary investigation to establish the universality of life. Take nothing for granted; constantly question information and those espousing it. Stereotypes and preconceptions will fall by the wayside. But more than that, the self will delve into a never-ending trip of personal exploration.

Spend periods of time alone in tranquil settings. Pray, meditate, or merely sit quietly. Concentrate on recently read material or search the inner realm for those characteristics that need improvement. This can be accomplished where the individual feels most comfortable, in an enclosed room or the external environment.

Priorities have to be rethought. Without a balance of the material and personal worlds, it is easy to get caught up in one or the other. Inequities are produced from an overemphasis on chasing wealth or pursuing truth. Some may find that they wish to concentrate on the spiritual side of life. Be warned, however, that one then must be prepared eventually to leave the planet permanently.

Seven Spiritual Qualities

To reach a state of completion, the individual should achieve a mental constitution that is personified by the seven spiritual qualities of being. They are intuition, knowledge, understanding, wisdom, counsel, courage, and worship. Through these a solitary person can meet all challenges.

Intuition is a direct awareness of something without conscious attention or reasoning. This fact or piece of information was not learned. No one else relayed it to the individual by voice, picture, or written language. It is instantaneous in occurrence. Clairvoyance, clairaudience, precognition, and retrocognition are examples.

Knowledge represents just the opposite of intuition. It is all the recorded and stored accumulation of human data gathered over a period of time. This information, while readily perceived to be factual, changes as it is updated with novel discoveries in the various fields of study. In the case of history, due to inaccuracies of biased perspectives (usually performed by conquerors or a prejudiced elite), much needs to be looked at anew. Life experiences contribute to knowledge as well.

Understanding consists of the sum of the mental powers by which knowledge is acquired, retained, and extended. In this way one can see the relationship between facts and make inferences from those correlations. Intuition is differentiated in that it takes little, if any, processing of information. People characterize it through symbology as a light going off in the head. Understanding also assists in appreciating others' experiences and views.

Wisdom is the ability to make practical applications of knowledge through understanding, which results in betterment or beneficial conditions. People move forward in their lives and advance their collective situation. This may refer to material distribution or usage at one level, and fair and selfless behavior illustrates it on another. Priorities and equitability also figure into such decision making. Determining all of these matters and others generally mandates considerable knowledge, but intuition has proven that certain people do not require extensive "smarts." (It is said that they simply know or are wise.)

Counsel relates directly to the latter, for it is the utilization of wisdom. Advice is exchanged mutually or guidance is provided for those in search of solutions to individual or social problems. Once again, in giving out possible suggestions for resolutions, either a great deal of knowledge (or experience) is needed or deep insight (intuition) has to be obtained.

Courage allows one to meet danger or opposition without fear. It is a strength of the inner self, when an individual shows firmness in his or her convictions (ultimately through absolute knowledge). A calm spirit, mind, and body (or balance in these three elements) provides the foundation to take a stand against extreme odds or external pressures.

Worship acts as the supreme ritual for connection to that which is larger than one's self. Whether it is done via prayer, meditation, or another procedure, this permits a person to merge with The All. In that way knowledge becomes absolute. Wisdom is acquired through intuition. Courage cannot be shaken. All preparations have been completed in order for a transformation to go forth.

Self-thinking, open education, and true knowledge are the basics for development. Once these have been achieved, the final phase begins. It will take strength of character to stand up for what one *knows* (not believes) is the truth. Suffering through ridicule and threats, plus a willingness to die to attain enlightenment, is the ultimate state of mind and being at the human level. By that time death consciously is understood to be a transition from one state to the next.

A specific destiny awaits each individual. The

potential each person possesses may or may not be fulfilled. Free will allows leeway to follow worldly enterprises and give in to the "deadly sins" that are a condition of humanness. Conversely, identifying personal capabilities and working to realize them is an additional viable alternative. No one should be derided for choosing either pathway. Each member of the human family is on a unique expedition that rests with the state of development of their spirit or essence.

Life circumstances furnish the setting for challenges with each return. These obstacles may be pushed aside or avoided, depending upon the attributes of the individual. The act of "growing up" continues. Nothing remains the same. Hard work is required. Just as schools and jobs exist for learning to open one's eyes to the human world, existence permits universal instruction to assist in comprehending the eternal macrocosm.

It does not come easily to everyone due to the extensive amount of time necessary to achieve perfection. Buddha once said that the process lasts as long as it takes a dove to wear down a mountain with only a scarf in its beak. Challenges and obstacles are the keys to learning and growing. Without them, stagnation would result. (Retired people who have no hobbies or nonwork interests fall into this trap.) Death follows shortly. Perfection can be accomplished only as the physical and then the emotional natures are mastered. Spiritual elements are left as the final ones to conquer.

The destiny of men and women lies beyond the universe of matter. As each spiritual essence reaches completion, it reunites with The All. This happens over and over again as all life forms fulfill their own evolution. When everything consummates total perfection, The All is the culmination of those endless processes.